OF BULLETINS AND BOOZE

OF BULLETINS AND BOOZE

A Newsman's Story of Recovery

Bob Horton

TEXAS TECH UNIVERSITY PRESS

This book is typeset in Times. The paper used in this book meets the minimum requirements of ANSI/NISO Z39.48-1992 (R1997). ♾

Designed by Kasey McBeath

Library of Congress Cataloging-in-Publication Data
Names: Horton, Bob, 1939- author.
Title: Of bulletins and booze : a newsman's story of recovery / Bob Horton.
Description: Lubbock, Texas : Texas Tech University Press, 2017. | Includes index.
Identifiers: LCCN 2016048475 (print) | LCCN 2017005198 (ebook) | ISBN 9780896729902 (hardcover : alk. paper) | ISBN 9780896729919 (ebook)
Subjects: LCSH: Horton, Bob, 1939- | Horton, Bob, 1939—Alcohol use. | Journalists—United States—Biography. | Alcoholics—United States—Biography.
Classification: LCC PN4874.H65 A3 2017 (print) | LCC PN4874.H65 (ebook) | DDC 070.92 [B] —dc23
LC record available at https://lccn.loc.gov/2016048475

17 18 19 20 21 22 23 24 25 / 9 8 7 6 5 4 3 2 1

Texas Tech University Press
Box 41037 | Lubbock, Texas 79409-1037 USA
800.832.4042 | ttup@ttu.edu | www.ttupress.org

For my sons, Bobby and Doug

Contents

Illustrations

Prologue

In 2015 Texas Tech's College of Media and Communications enrolled fifteen hundred students, some perhaps attracted by promises described on the college's website: "Change the face of advertising. Reach millions from the nightly news. Uncover the real story. Capture the world in photos. Mold public perception. Communications is all about passion." All are valid possibilities that can give a person access to icons of influence or wealth—connections tending to generate exaggerated ideas of self-importance. When I was growing up in West Texas I often heard what is probably a time-tested admonition about the danger of "getting too big for your britches." The hunger for success can lead one to swallow more ambitious notions than he is capable of digesting. Or, as a West Texas friend of mine once put it rather crudely: "Don't let an alligator mouth overload your hummingbird ass."

I was a news correspondent in Washington, DC, for almost a quarter of a century. During that time I was assigned to places most any eager journalist might wish to cover—Congress, the Pentagon, the State Department, the White House at times—all but, odd as it might seem in view of my rural upbringing in Texas, the Department of Agriculture. I met men of prominence, including five who were or would become president, a half-dozen who were in charge of the Pentagon or the State Department, leaders in Congress, and others who wielded levers of power in the federal government. I was no familiar face on television, but my byline appeared atop stories carried in hundreds of newspapers throughout the United States and around the world. Early in my career I received a national award for a reporting performance related to the assassination of President John F. Kennedy. Later, an Associated Press cohort and I were nominated for a Pulitzer Prize for our coverage of the Pentagon. Those were heady, intoxicating times, and I drank to celebrate my successes. I also drank to ease deep-seated fears that I was not only unqualified but also incapable of sustaining the charade for long. I drank my way into alcoholism.

The more I thought I achieved, the less secure I felt. I became obsessed with the idea that I had to outperform any other journalist reporting the story of the moment. I was my own worst competitor. I competed with a relentless notion that I always had to outrun the pack. Alcohol fueled the race.

Drinking became a routine occupying long lunches, resuming after work, and often continuing late into the night, when I might wind up gambling recklessly at poker in a game room at the National Press Club. I lost more than I won. I lost a devoted wife. I lost a sense of direction. I lost enthusiasm for a profession I believed was my true calling. I had arrived in Washington in January 1965 with a strong sense of being where I was meant to be. By 1989, however, I had changed jobs not once or twice but five times. I had lost that sense of being where I belonged. Something was wrong with the picture.

I eventually decided to remove myself from that place of monuments and monumental ambitions. Leaving Washington and all the promise it once held for me was painful, but Texas would welcome me home. I returned to the *Lubbock Avalanche-Journal*, this time not the rookie reporter I had been while a student at Texas Tech but as an editorial writer and columnist. Times were good. Times were bad. Most of the decade of the1990s was a repetitive cycle of drinking, sobering up, drinking again. By 1998 I had become so dispirited and incapable of dealing with an alcoholic behavior that I left the *Avalanche-Journal*. After drying out at a rehab facility I began living with my mother, who was nearing eighty in failing health. So began several years of sobriety benefiting both mother and son. She needed a caregiver. I needed daily meetings of Alcoholics Anonymous to abstain from liquor. I enrolled at Texas Tech and in 2003, at age sixty-four, I received a master's degree in mass communications.

Armed with the new degree I could have chosen to teach a younger generation what I knew about the news business. I was reluctant to pursue that path. I suspected—wrongly, no doubt—that I might be required to follow some paint-by-the-numbers lesson plan in a textbook written by an academic who had never been a reporter. If I were to lead a class of young people envisioning a sparkling career in communications or in any other field I would have my own firmly held thoughts to share. I might have little to say about alcoholism per se, but I certainly could emphasize that striving for success can be as intoxicating as the highest-proof booze and equally susceptible to an addiction.

OF BULLETINS AND BOOZE

The President and Mrs. Johnson
request the pleasure of the company of
Mr. and Mrs. Horton
at a reception to be held at
The White House
on Wednesday evening, May 18, 1966
at 7:00 o'clock

Invitation to the White House.

1

The embossed invitation that arrived with a Washington, DC, postmark on May 9, 1966, lifted our sense of social status well above the pleasant commonness exuded by the place where we lived in Rockville, Maryland, a few miles beyond the District line. The house was your average three-bedroom suburban brick, no fireplace, not carpeted, with a monthly rental charge of one hundred seventy-five dollars that stretched our pocketbook to the limit. The place was probably small enough to be tucked into a corner of the basement of the stately mansion of the people who invited us to drop by for a visit.

It was hardly a casual drop-by affair, as evidenced by the fancy script and imposing White House emblem that dressed the embossed card. I felt compelled to seek out my Amy Vanderbilt book-club reference on etiquette. What would an unpolished young Texan know about the proper way of responding to such a high-level *y'all come* beyond saying enthusiastically, heck, yeah, we'll sure as tootin' be there.

I drafted what I thought would be an appropriate letter of acceptance, learning later it was not necessary. A telephone call of acceptance to the White House switchboard probably would have sufficed. My wife and I weren't being invited to a formal White House dinner, which would have involved being reserved a designated seat. This was a lesser event, a reception at which we would pass in a receiving line to be briefly introduced to the president and first lady, then move on and wander about to see and be seen. It was nevertheless the most imposing official affair Sherry and I had the opportunity to attend in our first two years in Washington.

It was not our first exposure to the White House. One of the first things we had done upon arriving in 1965 for my move up in the news business was to play tourist and take one of the public walk-through tours of the place. At times during my initial night shift in the Washington bureau of the Associated Press I had been sent to stand outside the White House to watch for the president's return from some out-of-town appearance. The AP routinely reported a presidential homecoming with a sentence or two on the wire that was usually meant only as an advisory to editors. The purpose was to guard against being caught by surprise if Air Force One should turn up missing.

In my first months in WX, which was the AP's wire identity for Washington, I had no press pass to enter the White House grounds. A background investigation by the Secret Service is required before a reporter is granted a pass, and that takes time. Lacking the required credentials, I could only peer through wrought iron fencing to watch from hundreds of yards away for a military helicopter due to be ferrying the president home after Air Force One's landing at Andrews Air Force Base at Suitland, Maryland, a few miles outside Washington. As soon as a chopper fluttered down on the South Lawn, I'd call the office from a pay telephone that took dimes and say "he's back," even though I could only assume that the dark figures I could see stepping off the helicopter included The Man. Making assumptions is shoddy journalism. I was fortunate in those situations never to be burned by being wrong.

The invitation from "The President and Mrs. Johnson" was to attend a reception being held for US military commanders from around the world. In early 1966 I had become one of the growing number of newsmen assigned to cover news from the Pentagon, and we were included on the guest list. The White House undoubtedly had strong motive for inviting reporters. Willing or not, journalists often served as a conduit for conveying to the public the official rationale as to why expending blood and treasure in a distant war building in Vietnam was in the nation's security interest. Convincing Americans of the soundness of that rationale had become extremely important for the White House. Uniformed men and women were being shipped off by the tens of thousands to face bullets and bombs in Southeast Asia.

Public uneasiness about the growing numbers of Americans killed and wounded in South Vietnam posed a major political problem for

Cigar-smoking was not prohibited in the Pentagon press room (1966).

Lyndon Johnson as he looked ahead to a reelection campaign in 1968. Young Americans at risk of being drafted to fight in the jungles of Vietnam were marching in the streets, waving signs of defiance and derision toward a war many scorned not only as wrong-headed but even immoral. *Hey, hey, LBJ. How many kids did you burn today?* A speedy resolution of the conflict was needed to calm the turmoil back home. During a suddenly arranged visit to Vietnam, President Johnson told the troops he wanted to "nail the coonskin to the wall," which meant beating a Communist-backed insurgency that threatened stability in Saigon. He was relying on the military to get him out of a jam back in the States.

Sherry and I dressed in our Texas Sunday best for the excursion to the stately residence at 1600 Pennsylvania Avenue. A guard in a security booth checked credentials before pushing a button to open a gate to admit us onto the White House grounds. A curving sidewalk led us toward the towering white columns at the doors to the mansion. Inside, we joined a line of guests waiting to shake hands with President Lyndon Baines Johnson and Lady Bird Johnson. A man with a clipboard quietly asked for names, glanced down a typewritten list to confirm invitations, and, when our turn came, announced, quite regally, Robert Horton and Mrs. Horton.

Washington and especially the White House hold a powerful attraction for all manner of people beyond the Beltway encircling the District of Columbia. School children are brought from around the nation to see the marbled monuments and watch the robotic sentry march back and forth at the grave of the Unknown Soldier. An actor named Ronald Reagan comes out of Hollywood to play the role of his life as president in 1980. Elizabeth Taylor finds herself a US Senator as a husband. Major corporations assign their keenest minds to Washington to influence and even coerce the powers that be to shape legislation serving their commercial interests. And one day there we were, the son of an humble dirt farmer, and his wife, daughter of an oilfield worker, finding ourselves in the presence of the president and first lady of the United States of America. Truly, had we not arrived at a singular moment of prominence?

Lady Bird Johnson was smiling graciously as we approached our turn for the formal shaking of hands. Lyndon's eyes were half-closed as occasionally he reached over his shoulder to a mantle behind him to grasp a drinking glass with ice and what I surmised to be whisky.

Sherry modeled in Dallas and around Washington, DC (ca. 1966–67).

Sherry, quite the poised young mother and housewife, complimented Lady Bird on her dress. Lady Bird smiled and said something nice in return. Lyndon Johnson, a towering man, hardly looked down at me as we shook hands. He seemed bored with what for him was probably a tedious White House routine.

A combo played down the hall. Once the arrival formalities were out of the way, people were drawn toward the music in the Blue Room and began to dance. Sherry and I joined them for several turns out on the polished floor. Then, feeling more at ease, we began to explore the place, finding that we had virtually the run of the house but for the upper floor and the presidential couple's living quarters. Here and there stood nicely suited young men who might have passed as hotel bellhops instead of sentries. None interfered as we strolled about, imagining what life in such a grand place must be like. Unescorted, we walked down a stairway to the Presidential Collection Room, where china and silverware chosen for use by previous presidential couples were displayed on shelves and in gleaming settings on long dining tables. We learned from information cards placed here and there that Mrs. Woodrow Wilson created the room in 1917 to exhibit the growing collection of White House china. Before then, presidential china was regularly auctioned away for funds to buy new china.

The weather was warm, and we made our way out on the South Lawn, where tables with white linen were spread with big vessels of chili con queso, bowls of chips, drinks in plastic stemmed glasses, and spreads of hors d'oeuvres, or, as Lyndon the rough-speaking Texan supposedly called them, "whores doves." We nibbled. We sipped margaritas. We felt important.

With so many people of power and prestige on the scene, a great news story should have been there for the taking. There probably was, but it was over my head, literally. On a balcony overlooking the South Lawn the president sat murmuring quietly with three or four gentlemen, among them the longtime chairman of the Senate Foreign Relations Committee. Senator J. William Fulbright was a fellow Democrat of Lyndon Johnson and had worked with him closely over the years. But in the mid-1960s the two were at odds over the war in Vietnam. Fulbright had his committee conduct hearings on the issue. Voices of dissent toward LBJ's policy were aired nationally. Americans became polarized in their views about sending troops off to defend a weak, unpopular South Vietnamese government, even one threatened by a Communist regime to the north.

Had I been the enterprising reporter I felt destined to be, I might have sought out a back stair that would have led me to that lofty spot where Johnson and his companions were consorting, in my mind possibly making private accommodations with each other's views. Perhaps all I would have needed was to get past a distracted sentry. Perhaps another margarita or two would have emboldened me to step forward, ask difficult questions, and make front-page headlines. It was a brief notion not pursued, and probably wisely so. I myself might have become the news by being an inebriated reporter who got tossed off a White House balcony by the president of the United States. An alternative was to turn instead toward the tables on the lawn with their whores doves and salt-rimmed glasses. That became the less perilous notion. Another margarita. Three or four more for the good times.

A send-off to Washington from the AP in Dallas (1965).

2

Even when you're from Texas, where everything is reputed to be bigger than big, you still expect the first sight of such a celebrated place as the nation's capital to be awesome. The view did not affect me that way at all as we arrived in Washington on a sunny but crisp January afternoon in 1965 after a three-day drive from Dallas. The only thing that impressed me was how un-big the place appeared. There was hardly a skyline. There was not much *there* there. That was a bit of a letdown. I was supposed to be arriving on a bigger scene, the big time in the mind of any right-minded reporter.

I learned later that a law first passed in 1899 known as the Heights of Buildings Act prohibits any building in the District of Columbia from rising above one hundred ten feet, or about twelve stories. Nothing was to obstruct the view of such monumental edifices as the Capitol. Oddly enough, the National Press Building, where I would work nine years and three different careers later, did have a thirteenth floor. I heard that an exception had been made for that particular building, which houses offices of domestic and foreign news correspondents, public relations people, and lobbyists working the nation's capital. Or maybe the architects simply figured out a way to telescope thirteen floors within the hundred-twenty-foot limit.

If the size of Washington's buildings didn't impress me, the challenge and complexity of the AP operation where I arrived to work my first day that winter in 1965 certainly did. The AP's news operations were directed from a one-story building that could have been mistaken for almost any commercial business place in the heart of a downtown area, which is where it faced traffic passing along 1300 Connecticut Avenue.

The AP operation at that time was antiquated, measured against today's technological standards. The entrance to the AP office led past a manual switchboard where comely Mary Tuthill used pull-and-plug cords to connect incoming calls to whomever was being called. The dawning of a computerized telephone system had not yet arrived for the AP in the mid-sixties. Inside the newsroom itself were rows of teletype machines, maybe twenty in all, clattering noisily as they typed sentence after sentence, a word at a time, a letter at a time, on continuous strips of paper feeding off rolls as big as a muscle man's biceps. A copy boy went about stripping the machines of their continuous regurgitation of news stories, sports scores, weather reports, and messages from newspapers or other AP bureaus around the country in cryptic wire service fashion, such as this:

> WX
> Apc updater asap re status lbj west coast trip.
> Chronicle asking.
> FX

The strips of news had to be cut into smaller pieces, separated by content, and delivered to desk editors, who penciled them up for teletype operators for rerouting to other wires for dissemination to news clients in the AP's geographic regions: FX for San Francisco and the West, KX for Kansas City serving the Midwest, and AX for Atlanta and the South. Stacks of newspapers, handbooks, phone directories, and reference works and piles of tattered clippings and old AP stories made the place resemble the average newspaper office, only much larger. Cigarettes and an occasional cigar smoldered in ashtrays at the desks of some editors. No rigid environmental rules existed then to deter lighting up.

I came on the scene given the in-house position of night filing editor, an assignment as uninspiring as the title suggests. Marvin Arrowsmith was news editor and number two man to Chief of Bureau Bill Beale. Marv was liked and admired by the staff for his quiet, patient way of supervising people. He had been the AP's White House correspondent

Fresh face at the *Avalanche-Journal* (1959).

when Dwight D. Eisenhower was president; he himself had something of a presidential aura: silver-haired, dignified, gentlemanly. He had left the White House when John F. Kennedy became president in 1960. The AP used the change in the presidency to make a change of White House correspondents. Marv was being groomed to succeed older, less communicative Beale as WX's bureau chief, as eventually he did.

One of Marv's responsibilities, and probably one of his least favored, was to instill enthusiasm in new troops like me who started out performing mundane desk work. He surely knew that such beginning assignments hardly assuaged the desire of a newcomer to be sent right away to one of the frontline reporting posts such as the State Department, Congress, the Pentagon, or even the White House. In his quiet way, Marv cast the best possible light on my new role as night filing editor.

"You'll get to see all the Washington copy," he said.

And so I did. I saw reams of it, from the White House, the Capitol, the Treasury Department, the Supreme Court, wherever the AP had correspondents stationed in government offices around town. The bureau had a staff of sixty reporters and desk men, ninety percent of them men, and every one of them was older than me.

I soon saw a way to demonstrate my writing skills despite being planted in a routine copy-editing role. Joe Kane, the late-night editor, often needed someone to rehash an existing story for use in the next news cycle, which would in my case be for afternoon newspapers the following day. Afternoon papers would not want to publish stories identical to those already seen in the morning paper; I could earn a byline for the PMs by rewriting another reporter's piece. A well-done rewrite would have my name appearing above stories being printed nationwide, even around the world. I could be content with that exposure until the day I would be one of the frontline correspondents.

The array of teletype machines in the Washington bureau was impressive, but their operation was not a total mystery to me. I'd gradually been educated about the AP's means of disseminating the news in my earlier years. In the fall of 1957, when I was a freshman at a two-year college in Big Spring, Texas, I talked my way into a part-time job on the local newspaper. The *Big Spring Daily Herald* had a single AP printer that tapped out a limited assortment of state, national, and world news. I would read the wire between typing up high school sports stories, bowling league results, and an occasional feature assigned to keep me busy. Two years later, I moved upstate to a full-time job while finishing junior and senior years at what was then Texas Technological College. There, the *Lubbock Avalanche-Journal* had an "A" wire with a fuller mix of news than the state wire I'd seen at Big Spring, and a special weather wire.

After I'd left Lubbock to join the AP in Nashville in September 1961, I saw for the first time how wire service stories were processed. Teletype operators using keyboards punched coded holes into an inch-wide length of paper tape. That tape would be fed into a teletype transmitter that sent the story out to AP member newspapers and radio and television stations at the rate of sixty words a minute—not exactly the flash movement of the news that would be possible in the computerized era yet to come.

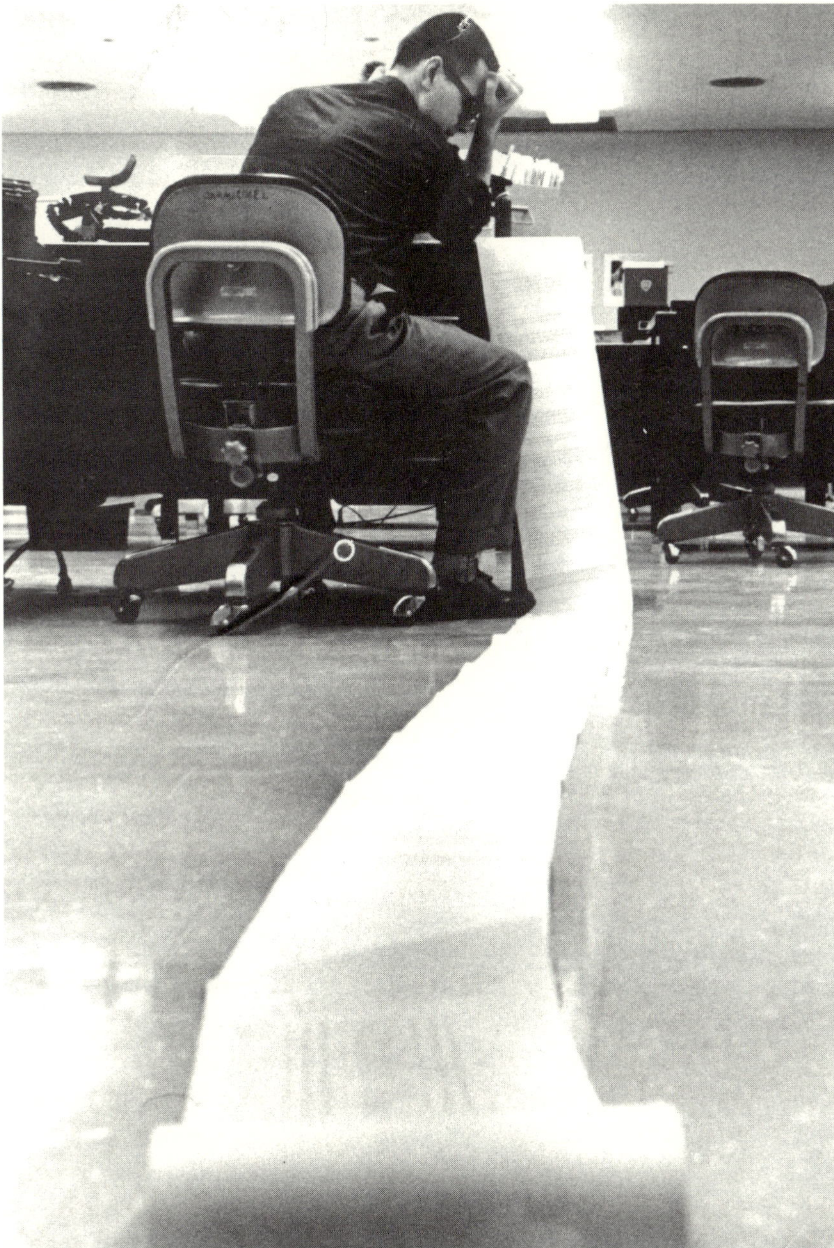

Attempting to write a shorter story at a desk in the *A-J* newsroom (1960).

Going airborne for the fun of it in the photo lab of the *Avalanche-Journal* (1961).

After three months of getting my feet on AP ground in Nashville, I was transferred to East Tennessee to be second reporter of a two-man operation in Knoxville. The AP had working space for me off to the side of the newsroom of the *Knoxville Journal*, a morning newspaper. The *Journal* was located upstairs in a building shared with the afternoon *Knoxville News-Sentinel,* a Scripps-Howard newspaper, on the floor below. There, Escar Thompson, the AP's World War II–toughened but kind and considerate correspondent in KV, taught me how to do the tape-punching routine myself. It was at first quite intimidating.

Once I had written stories using copy made available by the *Knoxville Journal*, I'd sit down at a teletype machine, punch the words into the coded paper tape, and transmit it onto the Tennessee state wire. If my Knoxville story was important enough to have regional or sometimes national interest, I would "schedule" its movement (*offer* is the more precise word) on the South wire by sending a message to AX, the regional distribution point in Atlanta. A sounding of bells on the teletype machine would alert me when Atlanta had an idle moment on the South wire. That would call on me to feed the tape into the transmitter and begin the printing out of whatever story I had "scheduled."

The trickiest part was learning not only to type but also to read the code of the punched holes in the tape so that, if necessary, I could erase and correct any errors in spelling. I learned the hard way that I should be careful not to step accidentally on the paper tape that uncoiled onto the floor as I sat typing. A crumpled tape would hang up in the transmitter and result in a stream of garbled letters on the printer . . . aiXQmr2lpxx-Zr . . . until Atlanta or whatever bureau I was sending copy to would take the initiative and interrupt the transmission. Embarrassing. I'd have to erase and swiftly repunch my tape or lose a turn at getting on the wire.

In the Washington bureau, teletype operators rarely had such problems. Most had been at their craft for years, quietly and efficiently processing each page of copy given them. Copy editors working with a pencil might have hastily edited words that were difficult to read because of indecipherable markings or misspellings. Some operators were confident enough and responsible enough to correct such things without having to consult with the editor. Their fingers danced on the keyboards as nimbly and as gracefully as those of a virtuoso stroking a Steinway. Good teletype operators made life easier for a night filing editor. They played a key role in moving the news swiftly.

I learned two essentials about wire service reporting from AP veterans who would become my role models. Get the story right. Get it out fast. The Associated Press had a tough competitor in United Press International. If a UPI man got his story out more quickly, that piece with his byline was more likely to get into the newspaper than an AP item arriving later. AP headquarters in New York kept close track of who was getting the "play" in newspapers that received both AP and UPI services. The AP log was mailed to outlying bureaus each week giving the numbers to reflect successes. A noteworthy performance by a staff member might bring an approving letter from AP headquarters in New York.

BH

THE ASSOCIATED PRESS
GENERAL OFFICE
50 ROCKEFELLER PLAZA
NEW YORK, N. Y. 10020

December 13, 1967.

Mr. Marvin L. Arrowsmith,
Washington.

Dear Marv:

The first chapter of Bob Horton's interesting rundown on the ABM developments got a fine ride in Sundayers. I enclose a random sampling. Quite a few papers broke the release and ran it the Sunday preceding, bit it doesn't appear to have daunted the others.

Sincerely yours,

RENE J. CAPPON
MANAGING EDITOR

AP in New York kept an eye on how well stories played in the papers.

As a newbie in the Washington bureau, I paid close attention to how good reporters operated. I learned that the best way to get the jump on a rival UPI man was to dictate a story from notes made at a news conference or briefing, rather than sit at a typewriter to tap it out. Experienced AP men could telephone a dictationist in the office and recite a story well enough to require little editing on the desk. Dictation was faster and also tended to force terse reporting, which often translated into greater clarity. Doug Cornell, who covered the White House for many years, was so accustomed to dictating stories that he found it too much of a chore to use one of the clunky old manual, upright Royals or Underwoods in the office. He once arrived at the downtown office after having covered an event away from his White House post and settled in a corner only steps from a dictationist at work under a telephone headset. From there he called the office switchboard, got a dictationist on the line, and proceeded to talk his story from the notes. Ten feet away, ten minutes, over and done, no sweat.

When finally I escaped the night filing editor role and was sent work daily at the AP's assigned desk in the Pentagon press room, I learned to dictate stories the way the big boys did it. Fred Hoffman, my AP cohort at the Pentagon, was among those who had become adept at reciting a story to a dictationist. My own ability to dictate from notes took practice, and in the beginning I doubted that I saved much time. I'd lose my train of thought about where I was in a story, or get hung up with clumsy phrasing. A patient dictationist sometimes helped me remember where my train of thought had derailed. Sometimes a better choice of word might be suggested in place of one I'd stuttered out. But over time I became better. And there were times the speedier dictation technique got my piece in the papers that were facing deadlines, leaving UPI's version the one to get tossed aside.

My first months as the night filer tended to be monotonous at times. The monotony was eased by a mid-evening break for refreshments that I began to enjoy with another staffer. Jim Munn was one of several AP men who worked on Capitol Hill to produce news for specific regions, but he too did his share of night work in the downtown bureau. Jim was a gregarious type, a good reporter whose assigned region included Minnesota, the home state of Senator Hubert H. Humphrey. Jim had a small claim to fame for breaking the news in advance of Humphrey's announcement in 1964 that he would be leaving the Senate to become Lyndon Johnson's vice president. On one of those monotonous nights, Jim told me how he often relieved the stresses of the evening by easing down to a hotsy-totsy bar at the Mayflower Hotel two blocks up Connecticut Avenue. He invited me to accompany him to indulge in a martini or two.

I knew little about martinis beyond having seen characters in movies sipping them from V-shaped glasses with tall stems. Recalling such scenes had prompted me to try my first martini during our high school senior trip to New Orleans in 1957. The concoction tasted like kerosene. The bourbon and Coke I'd learned to drink in high school at least had a sweet flavor. What was the big deal? One night in the Mayflower Hotel bar, Jim suggested that I specify having a Beefeater gin martini, and the experience was breathtaking. Crisp, clean, clarifying. Where the New Orleans martini failed the test, the Washington Beefeater was summa cum laude.

Lawdy lawdy lawdy.

So began a period of acquired taste for Beefeater martinis. Make it a Beefeater, I'd tell the bartender. Beefeater. I grew to like the sound of the word. I looked for opportunities to say it.

3

A story appeared in the December 17, 1966, issue of *Publishers' Auxiliary* magazine under the headline "Managing Editors Name Year's Outstanding AP Staffmen." The article in the oldest publication serving US newspapers was accompanied by a mug shot of a young man from Texas with a 1950ish burr haircut, looking solemnly through black, horn-rimmed glasses.

> SAN DIEGO, Calif.—The Associated Press Managing Editors Assn. has announced that AP Reporter Bob Horton of the Washington, D.C., staff and Photographer James Bourdier of Miami were winners of the annual APME awards for outstanding work by AP staffmen.
>
> The awards carry a $500 prize each for "top performance" during the past year. The prizes were presented here during the annual APME convention.
>
> Horton won the award for his reporting of a little-known episode that took place during the assassination of President Kennedy. Two years after the slaying, Horton told for the first time the story of the man who sat unobtrusively in the lobby of the Parkland hospital in Dallas as the president lay dying.
>
> The man, Ira D. Gearheart, was guarding a brown leather briefcase, sometimes called the "football" or "the message" or the "Black Box."
>
> Inside the case were the coded messages by which President Kennedy could order nuclear missiles and bombs against any ene-

> my. When President Kennedy died, Gearheart picked up the briefcase and strode past the emergency room desk into the surgery suite where, behind drawn shades, sat Vice President Lyndon B. Johnson.
>
> And with those footsteps, Bob Horton wrote, "came the first real, if not formal, transfer of presidential power."
>
> Horton's story appeared November 21, 1965, and it represented deep probing by the writer to discover who carried the briefcase and what his movements were as the president lay dying.

I had been in Washington with the AP only months when I wrote the story before being shipped over to the Pentagon. Many AP members across the nation used the piece, some with a cartoon illustration of a shadowy figure clutching the mystery satchel.

The "top performance" award boosted my confidence as a rookie newsman in Washington. That praise could have been a case of just a bit too much, too soon.

I had arrived in the nation's capital after barely four years with the wire service. Dallas was the springboard for a move up. In 1964 I had been a member of a special AP reporting team assigned to cover the trial of Jack Ruby for killing Lee Harvey Oswald, the accused assassin of President John F. Kennedy. I did not cover the trial itself. I did write sidebars about juror selections, about Ruby's flamboyant defense lawyer Melvin Belli, and about other goings-on outside the courtroom. Those stories went directly from Dallas to New York for distribution, which exposed my work to key AP people following "the trial of the century." An offer for me to go to Washington came within weeks of the verdict pronouncing Ruby guilty.

A few days before the managing editors' convention, a letter from AP headquarters in New York informed me I had been named to receive a "coveted award" from the AP Managing Editors. It was the only such award given to a reporter. Washington AP bureau chief Beale asked me to provide him some biographical information about myself, which was understandable. He supervised a staff of fifty or sixty newsmen, several of them former World War II correspondents. Because I was a newcomer, Beale knew little about me. I suspect he only wanted a few sentences about where I came from and what I had done before coming

BOBBY HORTON
Meadow, Texas
Guard 5'10"
Freshman

Basketball at Howard County Junior College, Big Spring, Texas (1957).

to Washington. I couldn't resist producing six typewritten single-spaced pages to tell him all about myself, beginning with the day I was born in 1939 when high winds were whipping ugly dust across West Texas. I proceeded to lay out my life story in excessive detail:

> When I was five we moved to New Mexico where my dad hired out for a construction outfit around Santa Fe. That was his brush with history. The project turned out to be the building of Los Alamos, the town being built in secrecy for the thousands of people who would be producing the first atomic bomb. My dad and the other workers sent to build houses and other structures had no idea what it was all about. He recalled noticing no smoking signs posted all over the place.
>
> Several years and a few farms later we were back at the same place

> I had started, Meadow, Texas. By the time I was a freshman in high school we were sharing the proceeds of our crops with my Grandad Horton, who had staked out one hundred sixty acres of land in Terry County around 1919.

I graduated from the small school at Meadow. My senior class numbered only eighteen. I was athletic enough to receive a basketball scholarship to Howard County Junior College at Big Spring, Texas, in oil country ninety miles south of Lubbock.

Two months after enrolling, I married a high school sweetheart. We lived in a snug upstairs apartment over someone's garage. Life was on the move.

I planned to go into the news business, but the two-year college in Big Spring offered no journalism courses. Nevertheless, one day I walked unannounced into the office of the publisher of the *Big Spring Daily Herald,* Robert Whipkey. I could see the skepticism in his face as I told him who I was and that I wanted to be a reporter. No, I had no experience, no journalism training, I said, but my high school English teacher praised my writing. I don't know why the man might have thought the paper could benefit by creating a small work role for me, but he did. One of the important moments in my life may have been when Whipkey asked whether I knew how to type. Yes, I did! Well, he said, let's see what we can do. After checking with his finance man, he decided that the paper could afford having me work fifteen hours or so a week. I could help the sports editor and perhaps eventually be out covering high school games when I wasn't playing husband, or student or athlete at Howard County Junior College. I would be earning a dollar an hour. It beat hoeing cotton.

Beginning with my junior year I transferred to Texas Technological College in Lubbock, where I duplicated what had worked for me in Big Spring, walking unannounced into the office of the editor of the *Lubbock Avalanche-Journal*. Now able to show some experience, I was hired. For two years I carried as many as eighteen hours of college courses a semester at Tech, maintaining a B average while working full forty-hour shifts a week at the paper.

In that extravagant biography prepared for my boss in Washington, I told about meeting AP's Dallas bureau chief, Bill Barnard, when he happened to visit at the *Avalanche-Journal*. I chatted with him as he lingered in the newsroom. Later I wrote him asking whether there might be a job opening in Dallas. Barnard must have informed AP personnel in New York about my interest. Within a few weeks of getting my diploma at Tech, I received a surprise call from Nashville asking if I would like to join the AP in Tennessee. I wanted the AP, but not necessarily Nashville. Still, I did not want to be stuck in wind-blown West Texas, so I accepted the offer.

Six weeks of becoming acclimated with the AP in Nashville led to two years at the AP bureau in Knoxville. In 1964, less than two months after the assassination of President John F. Kennedy, I was granted a transfer to Dallas, at my request. Sherry was pregnant and remained in Tennessee to have the child while I flew to Texas. She gave birth in a Knoxville hospital on the day of my first night shift in Dallas, on January 2, 1964. Knoxville boy Glen Douglas Horton was our second son. Number one was Bobby Don Horton, born on May 4, 1958, in Big Spring. Sherry and I had wed the previous fall when I first attended college on a basketball scholarship.

My Howard County Junior College teammates were surprised that I had slipped out of Big Spring and got married. Had they known, they'd have thrown a beery bachelor party. It was a lovely wedding at the little First Methodist Church in Meadow, my hometown. Sherry and I were as blissfully happy as a couple might be after a teenage romance devoid of any concerns about what might lie ahead. A summer of dating and dancing endures in my mind with all the loveliness of a fanciful fairy tale. A photograph preserves us smiling radiantly as we shared a knife to cut the ceremonial wedding cake.

So went my account for Washington bureau chief Bill Beale relating where I came from and what I'd done before joining the AP staff in the nation's capital.

•••

As 1966 spun out, I headed for the AP Managing Editors convention in San Diego. The air in the plane was as crisp and as cool as the blue of the new suit I'd packed for the occasion. It was the first suit I had ever bought. I sensed that life had taken a sweet turn. As it turned out, it may have been too sweet.

MR. and MRS. BOBBY LEE HORTON

Sherry Don Spears and Bobby Lee Horton wed in the First Methodist Church at Meadow, Texas (1957).

I had never been to the West Coast, but I became enamored with the idea that I should experience more than California. A little excursion to Las Vegas would add to the adventure. The award from the Associated Press Managing Editors Association came with that five-hundred-dollar check, and the AP itself had a policy of matching such honorary prizes. Since I fancied myself as something of a gambler, why not turn one good fortune into greater good fortune? Once in San Diego I made an excuse to Beale about visiting a friend in Los Angeles. He told me just to make sure to be back in time for the banquet. I promptly booked a flight to Nevada.

In those days there was no marketing bit about what happens in Las

Vegas, stays in Las Vegas. In my case stay it did. I went, lived it up for hours through the night playing blackjack and tipping cocktail waitresses handsomely, and returned to San Diego just before dawn with a maxed out credit card. Sampling the sweet life had been expensive, a lesson I would need to relearn time and again.

Short of sleep and somewhat shaky, I returned from Las Vegas to make the AP Managing Editors awards ceremony on schedule. The convention took place at the Hotel Del Coronado on the Pacific Coast, a lovely setting. Some advertising sharpster drew from the depths of his inspiration to write breathlessly how he saw it: "With its iconic red turrets piercing the taut horizontal lines of an azure California skyline, the Hotel del Coronado radiates with a confidence of gracious Victorian splendor that is without equal." Give the advertising sharpster a prize. Certainly it was the largest, most opulent hotel one country boy had ever set foot in. It was good that AP was picking up the tab. I couldn't have, not after Vegas.

On a pleasant Pacific evening I walked onto a stage where nice things were said about my assassination-day story, was presented with a nice plaque, and enjoyed nice applause. Later, at a cocktail event, several editors came around to congratulate me, among them Ben Bradlee of the *Washington Post*. I behaved as humbly as I should, being a novice journalist not long removed from Texas. All was good.

On the plane back to Washington I was seated with bureau chief Beale and Wes Gallagher, general manager of the AP in New York. More of those nice words were said, some about my work at the Pentagon, where generals and admirals were coping with a worrisome new war in Vietnam. Gallagher then said something that portended promise: "We may have other plans for you later." I came to think it was a hint that I was considered a candidate to replace one of the three AP correspondents assigned to cover the White House. There was no White House spot open, but Karl Bauman was nearing retirement. In the meantime, however, the Vietnam War was deepening, and so was my ability to write with growing confidence about ships and planes and men at war. I remained one of those reporters reporting a war from afar.

As it turned out, covering the Pentagon produced a more satisfying development than receiving the APME award. In 1968 AP New York proposed to submit a collection of our Pentagon stories to the committee deciding the next recipients of the Pulitzer Prize. I say "our" stories because I was paired with AP cohort Fred Hoffman, a savvy, no-nonsense reporter who had been sent across the Potomac to the Pentagon a year or two before I arrived. Fred and I assembled a number of stories and sent them along to New York. I don't remember the stories we chose to be nominated. No matter. When the Pulitzer Prize winners were announced, our names were not among them. It was nevertheless an honor that the AP considered our stories prizeworthy. Whether the White House assignment would have occurred if Pulitzer acclaim had come remains one of those what-ifs. Lessons remained to be learned—the hard way.

4

A black government car awaited my arrival at Andrews Air Force Base outside Washington at the conclusion of what should have been a routine press excursion to a military base late in 1968. A two-star general wanted to see me at the Pentagon. He, and others even higher than his lofty rank, had a problem with a story I had written about the US bombing campaign of the Vietnam war. Maj. Gen. William C. Garland, head of the Secretary of the Air Force Office of Information—SAFOI, the Pentagon's acronym for it—wanted to chat with me about the article.

I had flown with other Pentagon reporters to Eglin Air Force Base in Florida to hear about a new phased-array radar being built to detect Russian missiles. What I chose to write about instead had created a stir from the United States to Southeast Asia. Soon after arriving at the base, I had sought out a briefing officer who was knowledgeable about the special air operations in Vietnam. We talked, and the way I heard it, a secret bombing operation had been going on that in my mind had major political implications. People already were uneasy about the costs of Vietnam in lives and money. Any idea that the war was being expanded would not sit well with voters. I thought I had stumbled onto a story too good to be true. Eager to make headlines, I wrote it. The story aroused widespread attention. Unfortunately, it wasn't quite true. In reality, as I would determine over the years, it was true only in an oblique and irrelevant respect.

A telephone call awakened me early in the motel room where we reporters were staying. AP news editor Marv Arrowsmith was calling from Washington with unsettling news. The White House was publicly and emphatically denying that what I wrote was true. So was the State Department. The Kingdom of Bangkok issued a statement through the US embassy in Bangkok blasting it as false. Marv asked me whether I was sure about the soundness of the story, which I felt I was. The AP nonetheless was obliged to report the government's disclaimer, and did.

I sensed that I was in deep doo-doo. I felt uneasy being summoned to Air Force headquarters to hear what I suspected would be some rather harsh words. It might not involve being chastised the way Gen. George S. Patton slapped a soldier he thought was a malingerer in World War II, but I had no grounds for believing that the meeting I was about to have with the general would be a cordial affair. Nor was it. But it wasn't brutal.

The general was quiet, soft-spoken, businesslike: I was offbase, the story was wrong. I suspect that General Garland had been instructed by his boss, Air Force Chief of Staff Gen. John C. McConnell, to straighten out this AP kid. Even at twenty-eight years old I was pretty much a kid, military-wise. I'd never seen combat. My only exposure to the military before becoming a Pentagon correspondent came when I signed up for the Texas National Guard in Brownfield, Texas. I was at that time a seventeen-year-old junior in high school at Meadow. I joined because it seemed like some kind of neat club that several of my schoolmates also were joining. We dressed in olive drab like soldiers and practiced marching in a Veterans of Foreign Wars parking lot, shouldering ten-pound M1 Garand rifles that GIs had used in World War II.

"Whoever told you that was wrong," the general said by way of implicitly inviting me to divulge a name. I wasn't about to reveal the identity of the briefing officer. I suspected that people at the base knew or had reason to know who he was, although I could not be sure that was the case. I didn't want a career being ruined for someone's having told me "on background"—which is to say not for attribution—information classified as secret.

General Garland did not pressure me to write another story backtracking or negating what I had written. He knew that I had been around the Pentagon for some time. Information people are generally careful not to strong-arm or otherwise unnecessarily antagonize reporters who are regularly assigned to cover a beat. Those reporters, after all, are the important conduit for relaying the official line to the public. I told the general that the Associated Press had already reported the official denials of my story, and I left it at that. And so did he.

How did I get in such a bind? It could not have helped that the night before writing my controversial piece I'd consumed a dozen Gibson martinis at a reception thrown for us by a local Chamber of Commerce near the base in Florida. I recalled being a bit fogged and still tasting the salty cocktail onions of those Gibsons the next morning when I sat down to talk with my man at the base. Either I didn't hear clearly what he proceeded to tell me or he didn't make himself clear. In any event I was eager to come up with a story more interesting on the trip than a routine report about a fancy new radar. I was ripe to hype a story based on a shaky foundation.

In subsequent years I would try to uncover any information to confirm that a secret bombing campaign had been conducted inside Thailand as part of the US strategy of preventing a takeover of South Vietnam by Communist forces. I scoured hundreds of pages of congressional testimony by government officials in search of some clue or hint to satisfy me that I had not been wrong in what I wrote. I found none.

What I did discover was a bombing operation that did not represent what I had termed an expansion of the war—at a time when Lyndon Johnson was saying he wanted a peace settlement—but which did eventually turn out to be controversial in a different respect. The United States had begun using the poisonous Agent Orange over jungled areas to kill off dense vegetation that concealed North Vietnamese troops moving down the Ho Chi Minh Trail in Laos and eventually into South Vietnam.

If my briefer ever mentioned the word herbicide, it escaped my ears. He did not mention Agent Orange, which would have meant nothing to me anyway. Its development and experimental use elsewhere had been conducted in secrecy. What I did hear was that some C-123K aircraft had been brought into Thailand for use in a new air operation. In my mind, that translated into an expanded air war. But again, as I would learn belatedly, those new air operations did not involve dropping bombs on enemy forces inside Thailand. The Thai kingdom went to great lengths to conceal its assistance to Washington in the Vietnam war.

A dozen Gibsons at an open bar, an overzealousness to write the story no one else would have, an impatience about waiting until I returned to Washington to double-check what I thought I had learned—all factored into the makings of a bungled job of reporting. There was no escaping reality: My bad. For years the mere thought of the salty cocktail onions I'd consumed in those Florida cocktails turned my stomach.

5

I began life country to the corpuscle, plump as a pampered pup. The hour of birth itself wasn't so early, especially not for a couple who lived many years on one Texas dirt farm after another. You called it a dirt farm because often there was too little rain to justify calling it a cotton farm. Harvesting anything more than a small trailer load of gnarled bolls was a tough order of business. It involved getting out of bed at five or so, eating before the sun cracked the horizon, and mounting a coughing old tractor. Or going off to swing a hammer for a bit of carpenter's pay on the side.

The birth certificate pinpoints my arrival at 8:24 a.m., January 25, 1939. I wonder about its accuracy to the minute. Another entry on the document was not accurate, as I would notice years later. I was supposed to be Bobby Lee Horton, but the certificate had me come on the scene as "Bobbie." Heaven forbid. That made it sound as if I were a girl. For official purposes of the State of Texas I became Bobby only years later when my mother went to the courthouse to correct the birth certificate. I don't recall making an issue of being girlishly identified. Perhaps I did say something.

I'm certain that the error bothered her. Viola Faye Horton was a bright young woman who wanted things to be right. It wasn't right that she had to leave school in her freshman year to pull cotton during the Depression. She had thrived on school. She said she never understood why other students would say they looked so eagerly ahead to the weekend. She wanted to be in school—"I dearly loved it," she said. She loved books. She relished claiming blue ribbons in spelling and writing. One

Roy Winfred "Coonie" Horton and Viola Faye Horton with baby Bobby Lee (ca. 1940).

day she would want me to win ribbons, too. Her competitive nature became my nature, one day serving me well, other times frustrating me. I eventually learned that one doesn't win at everything.

Roy Winfred Horton was a quiet, supportive father who never pushed me toward any particular course in life. His watchful attitude did tell me that he wanted me to learn how he did what he did and to learn it well. He showed me how a tractor should plow a straight row in the field, how a cow is milked, how you mix the milk with windmill water in a tall, funnel-bottomed separator so that the cream would divorce itself from the diluted part and could eventually be drained from a little spigot to be churned into butter. Churning was a little chore my mother let me do. Daddy worked at times on construction jobs for money that wasn't coming from dryland farming. He showed by example how to hammer without bending the nail, how to saw a board in an unwavering line. I failed to learn all I should have learned from either of them.

The birth certificate listing Meadow as my birthplace was an exaggeration, if not another inaccuracy besides my birth name. I was actually born in Grandad B. C. Horton's farmhouse two miles north of the town and about a mile down a bumpy dirt road west of what is now US Highway 62-82.

As a scissortail might fly, Meadow is about twenty-five miles southwest of Lubbock. The town wasn't always there, however, and that is not to state the obvious. The handful of people who made up what could hardly be called a town had once been in another location in northeast Terry County. The settlement was originally called Primrose and was moved in the early 1900s to a site three miles east of present Meadow with a population estimated in 1910 at twenty-five. Seven years later, the post office in Primrose, or Old Meadow, as it is now referred to, was shifted to the town's current site to be alongside the tracks of the new South Plains and Santa Fe Railway between Lubbock and Seagraves. When I was a teenager driving an old Case tractor up and down the cotton rows of Grandad's farm, I used to watch as the train passed by, sounding the horn as it rumbled over the crossing. I often thought of where it might be going and where it had come from, and how exhilarated a person might feel being bound for distant new places.

Towns rarely move. Some families move more than others. Our family moved from one Texas farm to another, to towns in New Mexico and back again to Texas and around. My life would be marked by constant movement. I have snapshot memories of the earliest places. A shadowy room with a pulsing glow of light from a coal oil lamp. The sight of a father leaning forward in a chair to hear a voice through the static of a radio broadcast. The chill of splintery flooring under my bare feet in a two-room wooden shack when I might have been three years old.

Some history is preserved on four pages of simple handwritten lines my mother once gave to my younger brother, Joe, about her early marriage. Not resolved is how my father came to have the nickname Coonie. That was his lifelong identification to everyone except his par-

Grandad B. C. Horton (center) in east Texas (ca. 1920).

ents. Grandad and Mamagran Horton never called him anything but his middle name, Winfred. How he got the nickname remains a mystery. Mama said she never learned its origin. Was it because he was a smallish five foot eight or so and had black hair like a raccoon? As a young man did he have the quick movements of an animal, or was there some comic element to the tag? So far as I could tell, Daddy felt at ease with it. In later years when he built homes around Lubbock, his business card used the nickname for sure identification: R. W. "Coonie" Horton. People knew there was only one Coonie Horton.

The two were married on August 21, 1937. They exchanged vows in Clovis, New Mexico, because they couldn't get a marriage license in Texas. He was seventeen; she was sixteen. In Texas, couples had to be eighteen to be wed without parental consent. Roy Winfred Horton and Viola Faye Kennedy did not have the advance consent of parents—not that of my father's mother, for sure. They eloped. Friends drove them to New Mexico for a marriage that began with only love and hope. Returning, they lived for a time with her Grandpa Kennedy in a little house near the railroad tracks, a place within sight of the Horton place. Everyone knew Grandpa Kennedy as "Kid" Kennedy. I remember him as being a quiet, cheery-faced gentleman with a big white moustache who wore a black vest buttoned tight around his rounded midriff. He dipped from a brown, squat jar of Garrett snuff.

My mother said she had nothing to eat the entire day of their eloping except a candy bar, a single Baby Ruth. That was not her greatest discomfort, however. Running off to get married did not sit well with the Hortons. My grandfather Bert Horton was one of the kindest, most sweet-natured men I have ever known. That accounts for my dad's own gentle temperament. I cannot say such a positive thing about Grandad's beloved wife Belle, who we knew as Mamagran. As far as I could tell she never forgave my mother for running off to marry her baby boy Winfred. My mother said the old woman cried about it for two weeks. Throughout my lifetime I saw Mamagran act nothing but aloof toward my mother, who always respectfully addressed her as "Mrs. Horton."

It must have been Grandad Horton's acceptance of the marriage that made possible a meal at his house the day after Mama and Daddy returned from running off to Clovis. Daddy's sister Velma apparently served as hostess. My mother, in writings for my brother, sister, and me, made clear, in a terse comment, that her new mother-in-law did not prepare the meal. "Velma fixed a real good dinner," she wrote.

One place to live, then another. Wherever. Early on it was a twelve-by-twelve-foot shack beside an underground cellar next to my grandparents' farmhouse. That must have been extremely uncomfortable, given Mamagran's rejection of the state of affairs.

Soon my parents with little cherub me removed themselves two miles west down a hard loam road to a two-room wooden frame house that Grandad Horton called the Wiggington Place. That was where I first experienced guilt. Two years old, experiencing guilt? I don't recall a harsh voice, but a moment came when eyes were fixed on me in a way that seemed disapproving. Mama and Daddy stared down at me in the kitchen. I might have toddled toward them from the only other room, an all-purpose area with an unscreened front door off the living

The farmhouse north of Meadow where Bob was born, built by Grandad B. C. Horton about 1930, vacant in 2016 but intact. Fallen is an Arizona cypress that stood there for decades.

room that had space for a bed, a corner where clothes and extra bedding were dropped, and a blue-speckled pot where big people could pee and poop. Nothing precise in memory tells me so, but as I stood there I felt a warmth in whatever underthing I was wearing. Or maybe I was wearing nothing down there at all. Whatever. Suddenly I was beginning to dribble pleasingly on the floor.

Those eyes. That guilt. Me, peeing in a pinewood Garden of Eden.

6

I felt miserable departing Washington in 1967 on my first reporting assignment abroad. Flulike symptoms set in after I received a hurried series of typhoid, typhus, tetanus, and other shots required for travel overseas. The immunizations had me feeling achy and feverish by the time I boarded a Trans World Airlines jet bound for Greece out of New York's John F. Kennedy International Airport. An airline hostess served me other shots I hoped might anesthetize me nicely. Three swiftly downed miniatures of booze only made me woozier and prone to worrying about silly what-ifs, such as what if I should die on the high seas on my maiden foreign mission?

War appeared imminent in the Middle East, and I was about to find myself on the periphery of the action. In May 1967 hostilities between Israel and Egypt were approaching a flashpoint. The United States had sent an aircraft carrier into the Mediterranean with a supporting cast of other warships capable of wielding big guns if American interests in the region were threatened. The AP wanted a correspondent to be with our US Navy forces, and I was the man of the hour. I realized that being chosen was a vote of confidence in me, as I had covered the Pentagon for less than two years. It was more confidence than I felt in myself.

Amid the self-doubts arose the memory of a frightful childhood experience I'd had with deep water. When I was eleven years old, out on the landlocked plains of West Texas, I almost drowned trying to swim in a livestock tank. A teenage companion had pulled me to safety just as I felt myself sinking into an eerie, strangely comforting darkness. Seventeen years later that memory revived itself as I peered out the window of the TWA flight. We were out over the gray Atlantic, hours from land, and it occurred to me that if for some reason the plane should go down, and if anyone survived the impact, the ocean would eventually swallow up even the strongest of swimmers—if not the ocean, then some ravenous shark.

It was no time to toy with such sharky fears. I was more concerned with how I would perform on a reporting assignment likely to gain worldwide attention. I asked my TWA hostess for another miniature, downed it, and kept shivering. She draped a light blanket across my shoulders. With no one in the spacious first-class seat next to mine, I curled into a fetal position and dozed fitfully.

On June 5, 1967, a light, propeller-driven Navy plane ferried me from Athens to the aircraft carrier USS *America* two hundred miles out in the brilliant azure waters of the Mediterranean Sea. The first glimpse of the ship down through the clouds made my stomach roll again. From the air the flattop seemed the size of a postage stamp. We were going to land on that? But as we got closer, the carrier loomed on the water like a huge apartment building with a long parking strip. The vessel extended more than a thousand feet long, at some points rising thirty stories above the ocean surface. It actually did have more tenants than most hotels. Spread throughout it were some five thousand Navy people responsible for maintaining and operating eighty warplanes, missiles, and other armament.

I was not the only reporter hooking up with the carrier. I soon met up with two other newsmen I knew from the Pentagon press room. Neil Sheehan of the *New York Times* had covered the early years of the Vietnam War for UPI. Robert Goralski of *NBC News* had also reported from Vietnam in the mid-1960s. Soon twenty-nine of us media representatives were aboard the carrier, including reporters from England's BBC, Greece, and West Germany. *Life* magazine had a young photographer who was shooting pictures incessantly.

For once I wound up having no wire service competitor; UPI's Harry Stathos was on the carrier, but he became ill and was abed in the infirmary for days. His incapacitation gave me no lasting satisfaction. I knew later that I had been an inconsiderate ass for failing to fill him in now and then on whatever news we were getting on the carrier. Given his circumstance, his reporting would have always trailed mine in reaching news tickers back in the States. I had yet to learn that a reporter should do what he can to help a peer caught in a bind.

Whoever made the decision to allow media to be with the Navy in the Mediterranean timed things perfectly. We arrived on the USS *America* the very day news broke that Israel was attacking Egypt's air force as a prelude to taking control of the Sinai desert. I had been briefed before leaving the Pentagon that the United States expected any Israeli strike to be swift, and that turned out to be quite the case. In what became known as the Six Day War, the Israelis seized the Sinai as well as the West Bank of the River Jordan and the Golan Heights, which had given Arab enemies perfect gun positions for firing down on the Jewish state.

The outbreak of war heightened tensions on our carrier. A general quarters drill sent crewmen rushing to their battle stations. The captain announced that the ship was now to maintain a defense condition known as DEFCON 3, which is above the peacetime status of DEFCON 5 but short of the ultimate DEFCON 1 that occurs when there is an imminent or ongoing attack against the United States or its forces. We were briefed about what we could report from the ship using Navy communications channels; our reports would be scrutinized to prevent the release of classified information. We would not be allowed to report, for example, where US ships were operating in the Mediterranean lest that expose our forces as targets.

Neil Sheehan of the *New York Times* and I both objected to the idea that our stories would be subject to censoring. I do not recall exactly what I said. Given an exaggerated idea of self-importance, I may have expressed the supercilious notion that no one had the right to mess with my precious prose.

The commander of the US Sixth Fleet, Vice Admiral William Martin, advised people in Washington about our displeasure with the clearance process and how it would delay getting our stories back to our home offices. In a cable from his command ship, the guided missile cruiser USS *Little Rock*, Martin said: "None complained about delay in filing except Neil Sheehan of New York Times and Robert Horton of AP who have both consistently felt that any suggested change for accuracy was tantamount to censorship. This attitude has resulted in their copy containing some inaccuracies and Horton's usage of some indirect quotations out of context." Martin's cable to the Pentagon did conclude on a positive, all-is-well note: "Until this occasion, the relationship between the Navy and the press has been excellent, and all have expressed appreciation for information and background they have received on seapower, its importance to the Mediterranean and Southern Europe, and the ships which are required to maintain that power. It is not felt that the spirit of cooperation has been damaged in any way."

The Navy was in fact extremely cooperative. We were allowed generally unrestricted movements throughout the carrier. A public affairs officer was often around to answer questions, but no one monitored who we talked to or where we went. We were free to observe, write about, and photograph activities taking place on deck, including the launching and recovery of F4 Phantom fighters and other aircraft undergoing training operations. NBC's Bob Goralski and I occasionally climbed up to the bridge overlooking the deck to chat with the amiable skipper of the *America*, Capt. Donald Engen.

Two of the first stories I filed to Washington from the carrier made prominent headlines. One reported Admiral Martin's telling us that the task force was in the Med to take any action necessary to protect US interests in the region. Another widely used story reported about the task force's harassment by a Soviet destroyer that kept moving in and out of the carrier's formation, violating the "rules of the road" on the high seas. The harassment went on until June 7, when the admiral sent a message in Russian and English telling the Soviet intruder to get out of the way or else: "Your actions for the past five days have interfered with our operations. By positioning your ship in the midst of our formation and shadowing our every move you are denying us the freedom of maneuver on the high seas that has been traditionally recognized by seafaring nations for centuries." The message concluded: "In a few minutes the task force will commence maneuvering at high speeds and various courses. Your present position will be dangerous to your ship as well as the ships of this force. I request you clear our formation without delay and discontinue your interference and unsafe practices." The Russian skipper heeded the warning and left, but other Soviet ships remained

Caricature of the Pentagon reporter covering war in the Middle East (1967).

close by, including a worrisome submarine that would figure in a graver crisis to come.

That moment of crisis came the next day, June 8, 1967. Bob Goralski and I were on the bridge visiting the captain and idly looking down on the deck at crewmen going about their midday activities. F4 Phantom fighters had been launched on routine training flights. Suddenly, I heard a voice crackle on Engen's radio, uttering words that were clipped and hurried. I thought I heard something like "we've taken hits." The captain turned and politely told Goralski and me to leave the bridge. On the way out I thought of the Soviet submarine that had shadowed the task force. The sub was being tracked on sonar by a destroyer of the *America*'s task force. Questions arose in my mind: Had the submarine torpedoed one of our ships? Had we hurled a devastating depth charge at the Soviet sub, creating a potential for war?

Momentarily we heard the captain's voice announcing over the ship's piping system that all aircraft on training missions were to return to the carrier as quickly as possible. A No Visitors sign went up outside the entrance to the bridge. Soon planes loaded with missiles were being rolled out and sent aloft. It seemed obvious that we were ready to engage someone in battle somewhere because of some grave occurrence. The scenario had developed so quickly and seemed so surreal that a frightful thought occurred: Could I be witnessing the beginning of World War III?

In a makeshift press room below deck we began to get fragmentary news from Washington that a US ship that was not part of our carrier task force had been attacked off the Sinai peninsula. Many crewmen were killed, many wounded. Why their ship was in that area and who had attacked it was a mystery. We were told only that the USS *America* would churn at top speed to the rescue of a ship called the USS *Liberty*.

Jane's Fighting Ships is a standard reference book that provides detailed profiles of warships of every nation. The 1966–67 issue of *Jane's* described the *Liberty* as a technical research ship, which might lead one think that she cruised around studying ocean formations or exotic aquatics of the deep blue sea. That was not exactly so. The *Liberty* performed "research in communications and electromagnetic radiation," a euphemism commonly understood to mean "intelligence collection." The *Liberty* was a mobile listening post capable of catching whatever electronic communications were in the air, provided the ship got near the source of dissemination. Would that be considered spying?

Overnight we learned virtually nothing worthy of reporting from the carrier. All news was being handled out of Washington, including the shocking revelation about the identity of the *Liberty*'s attacker: Israel, our ally in the Middle East, came forth saying its planes had attacked the ship by mistake. Tel Aviv was apologizing for its "tragic error," but as details came to light, the claim that the attack happened because of pilot error began to sound phony. The *Liberty* had been flying an American flag. Crewmen on the ship recognized the planes as Israeli and were out on the deck casually waving as Israeli Mirage-III fighter-bombers made initial passes overhead before returning to begin bombing and strafing them. The air attack was followed by an assault by Israeli gunboats that torpedoed the *Liberty*. Thirty-four US seamen were killed and one hundred seventy-one wounded, the worst loss of American naval people in hostile action since World War II. Somehow the *Liberty* remained afloat. The carrier *America* set forth at full speed to meet the crippled vessel in order to take on its casualties.

The next morning I was walking in one of tight passageways, wondering what I might file to AP WX about the attack on the "technical research ship." A crewman approached, said good morning, and paused to chat. He recognized me as one of the many reporters seen about the carrier. He had just come from night duty in the communications unit, he said. Naturally I asked about the *Liberty*. He explained that the ship had left Rota, Spain, earlier to reach a point near Egypt to be able to overhear radio communications. The United States needed know what was happening if and when war between Israel and Egypt broke out.

My conversation with the crewman was brief and just that casual. I didn't ask his name and never encountered him again. But on the way to a typewriter back at my sleeping quarters I decided what I would report and how I would categorize the *Liberty*. In my mind it could be called a "spy ship."

I knew that a story calling the *Liberty* a "spy ship" was unlikely to get past Navy officers who had been assigned to check all copy presented to them for transmission to our offices back home. So I bypassed the security clearance people. I tucked the story in a parcel to be flown to the AP office in Athens by a carrier onboard delivery plane like the one that had ferried me to the *America* at the start of the trip.

I didn't learn until after returning from the Mediterranean how my characterization of the *Liberty* as a "spy ship" had upset people at the Pentagon. The chairman of the Joint Chiefs of Staff, Gen. Earle Wheeler, was livid, I was told. I don't know whether he was angry at me—I had interviewed him on other matters not long after taking the Pentagon beat—or at the seaman who had talked to me about what the Liberty had been doing.

Over the years I lost the original copy of what I wrote. But the gist of it appears to be accurately reported in *Attack on the Liberty* (Simon and Schuster, 2009), written by investigative reporter James Scott. His father was an officer on the bridge of the *Liberty* when it was attacked. The book said:

> Another example of the Navy's unease centered on a story filed the day after the attack by Associated Press reporter Bob Horton. The reporter quoted an unnamed officer on the *America* who stated that the *Liberty* was loaded with eavesdropping equipment and tasked to spy on the Middle East War. "We moved in close to monitor communications of both Egypt and Israel. We have to. We need to be informed of what's going on in a matter of minutes." The quote sparked a secret investigation to uncover whom Horton talked to and how he fooled the Navy's minders. The results did not please the brass. Reporters typically filed stories using the carrier's teletypes. But Horton smuggled his scoop off the carrier on a routine delivery flight to Greece. "Mr. Horton's copy was not submitted for review or accuracy and it was not transmitted by Navy communications," stated a telegram. "It is believed to have been sent ashore in a sealed envelope placed together with other media materials."

After my story appeared on AP teletype printers around the world, the commander of the Sixth Fleet responded with a strong rebuttal. Admiral Martin said the *Liberty* had taken up position in international waters off the Egyptian coast "to be available for an evacuation operation should it be ordered." Any embassy or consulate with an emergency involving Americans would be able to contact the *Liberty* for assistance. As for the *Liberty* being a "spy ship," he said: "I emphatically deny it. I emphatically tell you that we were there to be a communications guard in case we had to mass evacuate."

Perhaps I deserved to have my knuckles rapped for labeling the *Liberty* a "spy ship." I saw it as an appropriate substitute term for the average reader for the label "technical research ship." James Ennes, who was a lieutenant on the bridge of the *Liberty* the day of the attack, has contended in his book, *Assault on the Liberty* (Random House, 1990), that Israel wanted to keep the ship from monitoring radio traffic that might show Israel as being the aggressor in its impending invasion of Syria, which the White House opposed. So—. Monitoring? Overhearing? Or spying?

As the carrier USS *America* neared the *Liberty* on June 9, the sight was appalling. The ship was pocked with scores of gaping black holes, shot up like some clunker in a junkyard riddled by buckshot the size of baseballs. It listed severely in the water; how it managed to remain afloat was amazing. Hundreds of *America*'s crew watching from the carrier's deck sent up a tremendous cheer as we drew alongside the battered ship. I had begun taking pictures with a small eight-millimeter Kodak movie camera as helicopters landed on the carrier with *Liberty* crewmen. Some were able to walk. Others, with shredded clothing exposing bloodied wounds, had to be carried. Several were laid out on the deck in rubber body bags.

Many in the United States rejected Tel Aviv's claim that Israeli pilots had attacked the *Liberty* in the belief that it was an Egyptian warship. Dean Rusk, who was secretary of state at the time, would say years later that he was never satisfied with Israel's explanation: "I didn't believe them then, and I don't believe them to this day." Others have said that Lyndon Johnson's White House went along with a cover-up of what really happened so as not to alienate Jewish supporters. Johnson's secretary of defense, Robert McNamara, told Congress on July 26, 1967, that an investigative body headed by "an admiral of the Navy in whom we have great confidence" had found that the attack was not intentional. McNamara continued to say years later that he had seen nothing to change his mind that there had been no cover-up. Both authors Ennes and Scott cited evidence they said showed that investigations into the attack were a whitewash.

With the conclusion of the Arab-Israeli war on June 10, tensions eased from the Navy's perspective. Before I left the *America* nine days later, the carrier set up a boxing ring in the hangar bay for a dozen fights between various people on board, no newsmen among them. Two thousand crewmen roared and cheered as their buddies slugged it out. Bob Goralski provided the blow-by-blow on the ship's TV system for those remaining at their stations. Some of the liveliest responses from the men came when a sailor went toe-to-toe against a member of the Marine detachment aboard the ship. I found myself standing beside one closely sheared Marine who turned crimson in the face screaming, "Kill him! Kill the g—damned mother-f—r! Kill him!" The rage could have been more intense only if his buddy's opponent in the ring had been an Israeli.

I left the *America* after nineteen days, returning home in time for the Fourth of July holiday. Home was now in Arlington, Virginia, where we had moved from Maryland so I could have a shorter commute to the Pentagon. Actually, it was no commute at all, barely a mile, which I would walk when the weather was pleasant. We were happy to be together again, my lovely wife Sherry, young Bobby and Doug, and me. I was ready to decompress from the Mediterranean experience, and so was Sherry. She had been anxious about my being in what sounded to her like a war zone. WX news editor Marv Arrowsmith thoughtfully kept her informed about what the office was hearing from me at sea.

Soon we headed out on the highway to visit our friends Everett and Katy Groseclose in the New York area. All four of us had worked at the *Lubbock Avalanche-Journal* during our Texas Tech eras. Everett, Katy, and I had been general news reporters; Sherry had been a proofreader. Everett was entering the Army as I left Lubbock to join the AP. After Army service he joined the staff of the *Wall Street Journal* and eventually wound up in New York. It was a pleasurable journey, traveling to our friends' home in Ridgewood, New Jersey. The radio dial turned up one station after another playing songs from a new, highly anticipated album by the Beatles called "Sgt. Pepper's Lonely Hearts Club Band." The sun was hot, the day was bright, and I felt reassured about how I had handled my assignment in the Mediterranean. News clippings from around the world showed that my stories were used extensively. Excerpts quoting "AP Reporter Bob Horton" often turned up in pieces written by others about the Six-Day War in the Mideast. I got by with a little help from my friends.

7

I was a good kid, I was a bad kid. I had some smarts, I also behaved stupidly. As a young boy I listened carefully to teachers; I looked up to coaches and tried to do what they taught me about football and basketball. Why then did I pull so many dumb stunts?

I'm nine, maybe ten, running as if my tail is afire, which I'm afraid it soon might be at the hands of a father, who is off carpentering. Behind me down a narrow dirt road that separates an expanse of wild mesquite from our field of pathetic dryland cotton something else already is ablaze: a two-wheeled trailer sprouting flames.

Had I thought of it later, I might have tried claiming that a bolt of lightning had suddenly flashed from the hard blue September sky. Would they have believed it? Maybe because I had been a somewhat spiritual young boy it never occurred to me to blame God. I often knelt alone in a barn and said the Lord's Prayer as I thought I should, no one knowing except the cow and me. On that hot September afternoon the truth would soon be known: God was not the arsonist. The guilty party was a kid who should have been on his knees in the dirt, not in prayer but head down stuffing cotton bolls into a canvas sack to help fill the trailer.

I had become bored. I found a book of paper matches left alongside the trailer by some other hired cotton picker. I had struck one of those matches and thoughtlessly—I am being truthful here—*thoughtlessly* touched the flame to a single strand of lint dangling between the wooden ribs of the trailer. Nothing flared at once. Instead, one spark leaped from one strand to another, something like a lighted fuse, until a spidery web of tiny flashes began to spread into and over the puffy mound in the trailer. Gray wisps of smoke caught my eye. I smelled trouble.

My brother Joe, three years younger than I, remembers what happened that day after school when we were out pulling cotton as our dad had directed us to do. "I had not finished my row, and you were up in the trailer," Joe said when I asked for his recollection years later. "I looked up and there was a lot of smoke and you were hollering 'Help.' You were throwing out cotton, and it was getting worse. We both ran to the house crying."

From somewhere came a car trailing dust as Daddy raced to pick us up running on the sandy turn road. We drove back to the scene of the crime in time to hear one of the trailer tires explode from the heat. The fire was rendering to ash and floating soot the load of cotton our family needed to help buy food for the table. Worse still, the blazing trailer wasn't even ours. It had been loaned to us by a kindly old neighbor a field away.

I have no recollection that my dad berated me. If he had any cross words, I must have blanked them out. Nor did he set my tail afire. The guilt I felt might have been assuaged had he taken the belt to me, which he was prone to do for lesser misbehaviors.

The question is an old one that lingers: I knew what I was doing, but what was I thinking?

Then came the time when a calf fell dead at my feet. The young animal died because—. Confess I must and will. I murdered that innocent young suckling. Innocent, yes, but also deserving, the stubborn little bastard.

One of my chores on our farm in the Union Community of Terry County was to milk the cow before sunset. The old cow we called Florene had a calf. The routine was for me to let the calf suckle for a few minutes, then pull the little bugger off using a rope around its neck, tie the animal to a post away from Florene, and then set myself on a three-legged stool to finish milking what was needed for the family.

On this particular evening—I might have been eleven years old and the calf was growing bigger and stronger by the day—I didn't have the strength to pull it away from sucking at Florene's teats. An idea came: if I stuck my hand inside the critter's mouth and gave a hard jerk on the frothy cheek, the animal surely would yield. One jerk didn't work.

When I tried a second time, the calf must have sensed my finger to be a fifth teat and chomped down hard.

Dang, that hurt! Dang, was I pissed! Looking around, I saw a rock, picked it up, and hurled it at the calf. The rock bounced away harmlessly off its back. Thoroughly frustrated, I grabbed up the rock again and threw it as hard as I could at the furry head bobbing and butting at mama cow's udder. The rock struck at exactly the right spot, dead against the back of the calf's head. The legs buckled. The calf went down immediately. I stood back for a moment enjoying a feeling of sweet revenge until I noticed that the young animal was not moving.

Florene's neck was braced in a V-shaped stall, where we placed her to munch feed from a trough while someone did the milking. Sensing that something had happened to her offspring, mama cow suddenly began bawling and pawing her hooves in the dirt. Alarmed, I did the only thing I knew to do, which was run to the house, where supper was being served, and exclaim in the most puzzled tone I could manage, "Daddy! There's something wrong with the calf!" I was dead right about something being wrong. Our young suckler out in the barn was dead. Dead as a doornail, whatever that means. I used to hear my dad say it a lot.

Once again, as with my igniting a trailer load of cotton, my dad listened without obvious anger to my explanation about what happened. He may have lit a cigarette, but it didn't take long for him to decide what had to be done to prevent a dumb deed from being a total loss. As sunset bled into darkness, he strung an electrical cord out to the barn, hung it over a rafter, and switched on a light bulb to see what he would be doing. A braided, three-strand rope looping from a rafter soon had the calf suspended by the hooves, head down. Armed with a butcher knife, he thrust blade into fur and proceeded to skin the animal, gutting it and slicing away slabs of meat for a deep-freezer back at the house.

For months after the night of bloodletting in the barnyard, our supper table had good servings of chicken-fried young calf. It was delicious, the way Mama cooked it, even if I couldn't always forget what it was that I was eating.

There were far more times of pleasant calmness than crisis on that farm where we were living in 1948. We had little to do in the evenings after supper. We had radio but no television for entertainment. Television didn't exist for us until KDUB-TV started broadcasting from Lubbock in 1952. Rural Free Delivery brought advertising circulars and a monthly magazine or two to the mailbox to look over. On summer nights I'd sit outdoors listening to the insects buzzing in the darkness, the windmill creaking in a slackening breeze, and try to spot Orion's Belt and other asterisms in the heavens. Mama and Daddy began bringing out a deck of Bicycle cards to teach my six-year-old brother Joe and me games such as Rummy and Casino. That was quality time for the family before the term ever existed. Mama loved shuffling the deck, explaining the rules as she flipped out the cards, and winning. She'd laugh when she won a game, or even a single hand, and that made me want to win so I could laugh, too.

My mother had a motive for seeing me succeed that went beyond her living vicariously through the achievements of a son. She checked my report cards carefully to see that I was making good grades. She wanted me to get an education and, as she sometimes said, grow up to be somebody. I know now that she meant that I should be somebody besides a farmer. She loved her farmer husband. She just couldn't see a future in it for me.

The destiny she chose for me was to become her little award-winner. Trying my best, I did win small honors. On May 19, 1948, the superintendent of the Union School District, along with the principal and my fourth-grade teacher, signed their names to a certificate of award for me "for achieving high honors in all subjects." Rarely throughout school years did a report card of mine show a grade other than an A. Later, when I was in the eighth grade at Meadow, the *Brownfield News* had a front-page story with the headline "Bobby Horton Is Winner of County Spelling Bee." A double-column picture showed me receiving a twenty-five-dollar cash prize that accompanied the award.

By the time I was a senior at Meadow, which had a high school enrollment of about fifty students, I had won several University Interscholastic League events. The University of Texas had created the UIL in 1910 to provide "educational extracurricular academic, athletic, and music contests" for public school students. As a sophomore I won my district's event in "ready writing," which involved writing an essay on a topic chosen from among five possibilities offered the contestants. In the regional round at Lubbock, I qualified for state and placed third at Austin. My picture appeared again in the Brownfield paper.

Achieve little victories and people expect bigger things. They speak about how you have "potential" and can achieve even more. No one, however, really defined for me what that "potential" business meant. If there was a pinnacle for reaching your potential, where was it to be found? The latest achievement created pressure to achieve something even more impressive. The key to succeeding as I understood it meant competing, and I learned to compete hard. Giving it all you've got was supposed to get you where you wanted to be, so I was led to believe. What I did not grasp was a reality: You never win it all.

Flash forward to a time in 1957, and I find myself rationalizing how we lost a state basketball championship that could have been ours. We had arrived at the gymnasium on the University of Texas campus as one of the most confident teams in the high school playoffs. We'd lost to only one team all season (although it happened four times in nonconference games against archrival Ropes High School, just up the highway from Meadow). Little Meadow High School had never before qualified a boys basketball team for the state tournament, much less had one appear in the championship game. History was riding on our shoulders. Unfortunately, by the time the state championship game was tipping off we were, in the words of good ol' West Texas boys, scared shitless. In my mind several things happened that set us up for a devastating defeat. The bad weather. Coach Charley Rand's inability to get to the game on time. My fouling recklessly. Game referees' watching me too closely. My mother's teaching me to compete too hard. All that and, well, yes, a tough opponent.

Turbulent weather delayed Coach Rand's showing up for the game until we had already been playing for several minutes. He'd flown to Canyon in the Texas Panhandle that morning to coach the Meadow girls' team in a regional semifinals game. A chartered plane was to have gotten him back to Austin in time for our one o'clock tip-off. A rainstorm stalled the landing.

A sickly feeling welled in my stomach when we got word in the dressing room that we would be taking the court without a coach. Surely something would be done to prevent our being leaderless, I thought. But four other championship games involving the larger schools were to be played after we led off the day in UT's old forty-four-hundred-seat gymnasium, so officials would not upset the schedule by delaying the

Selected with senior classmate Sue Fulford as best athletes (Meadow High School yearbook, 1957).

start of the smallest schools' title game. Gilbert Bell, our big-scoring center, and I were the only senior starters. We'd played together for four years. We had more experience and therefore more poise than our younger teammates. Yet neither of us had ever felt so unsettled and unsure of ourselves at the outset of a game.

As soon as the game tipped off, a competitive nature nurtured by my mother for once became counterproductive. I started out playing too aggressively, fouling recklessly. Narrow-minded referees assessed me with four fouls in the first half. One more foul and I'd be bench-bound. Coach Charley Rand arrived to cheers midway in the first quarter. By then we were behind 11 to 4. After halftime he kept me on the bench with my four fouls. I was sent back onto the court later in the third quarter, and we cut the deficit to five points. But the refs who had been watching my overzealous defending tagged me with a fifth no-no. What an inglorious ending to the final game of my senior year. As the clock ran out, I peeked from under a towel over my head and saw the result in numbers too bright to accept: 80 to 59.

Dreams of a state championship had been blown away like a tumbleweed in a West Texas dust storm. How embarrassing. And in a way how ironic that the team that thrashed us so soundly should be from a school named Big Sandy. An imaginative sports writer could have had fun with the headline: *Big Sandy Blows Over Meadow.*

As the last days of May 1957 carried us to graduation, life as I had known it was over. Glory days had ended. Over the years I would have a recurring dream that I wasn't really a senior the year of the debacle, that the next year we'd all be back on the court stronger than ever. We would emerge champions in that final game in Austin. It was, of course, only an illusion. The reality I needed to learn is that success can come in different forms.

8

The news desk at the AP office downtown rang me at the Pentagon late on a Friday afternoon. I had a message to call a certain agent named Whitehead at the FBI. Call who at *where*? There was no explanation as to why. I didn't know an agent named Whitehead. I hadn't written any bad checks or pilfered any federal files. As far as I knew I hadn't been involved in any criminal activity that would have caught the FBI's attention. Still, knowing that a federal sleuth was looking for me did not seem to be the best way to start my weekend.

Agent Whitehead was gone for the day. I told the woman answering the FBI switchboard who I was and that the agent had tried to reach me. She said she would take a message. Agent Whitehead would probably get back to me Monday.

Monday would not do. I did not intend to spend Saturday and Sunday wondering why the FBI wanted to talk to me. I asked the switchboard person—told her—please get word to Agent Whitehead that the AP reporter he was trying to reach wanted to talk to him. The FBI always gets its man. Turnabout is fair play; I wanted to get my man. FBI lady said she would pass along my request. I was at home an hour later when Agent Whitehead called. He was friendly. He told me briefly what it was all about. They wanted to know about my dealings with the Russian.

Oh. The Russian.

I was ready to talk on the phone, but Agent Whitehead said Monday would be better. He wanted to come to the Pentagon, get acquainted, and chat. It never occurred to me to tell him that who I talked to as a newsman was not the government's business. Some reporters might have taken such a position, based on the principle of Freedom of the Press. But refusing to talk to the agent would have left me wondering why the FBI should have any interest in my dealings with the Russian. So I agreed.

It evolved into a good cop, bad cop routine when we sat down to talk Monday in a room normally used for Pentagon press conferences and briefings about Vietnam War issues. Agent Whitehead came with a dour-looking partner who kept intruding in what I thought would be a one-on-one situation.

The FBI was aware that a correspondent for the Soviet news agency TASS had been coming to the Pentagon to attend sessions for the press. The Soviets had an embassy in downtown Washington, but the agency was curious about why they would be sending a man across the Potomac to sit in on what were usually humdrum press events producing little news. Regulars in the Pentagon press room attended them mostly out of a sense of duty and for lack of anything better to do. But this was in the late 1960s with the war going on in Vietnam. One never knew when Washington would open up with something about the war worthy of headlines.

The name might well have been Boris or Ivan, I do not remember. I recall that he was young, perhaps in his mid-twenties. He was dark-eyed and darkly intense, perhaps as you might expect of someone who felt it necessary to be cautious about where he was and how he might be perceived. I think many of us suspected that any TASS correspondent could be an intelligence agent or have at least some information-collection function as part of his Washington assignment. Reporters being reporters, we were as curious about him as he was about us.

Whitehead somehow knew that the TASS man had introduced himself around the press room where we regulars had government-provided desks and typewriters. At one end of the room AP cohort Fred Hoffman and I had a telephone to our office downtown as well as a Pentagon phone that gave us access to offices within the US defense system. Near us was former *Wall Street Journal* reporter Bill Beecher of the *Boston Globe*. At the far end of the room were the *Baltimore Sun*'s Henry Trewhitt, and close by him UPI's Charlie Corddry and Steve Garwood. Out in midroom sat an affable Texas associate of mine, Hugh Lucas, who reported for aviation and aerospace publications. Other Pentagon-accredited reporters from major newspapers such as the *Washington Post*, the *New York Times*, and the *Los Angeles Times* had assigned desks as well, but they tended to come and go as news situations warranted.

I was unable to tell agent Whitehead which of my fellow journalists had been approached by the TASS correspondent, but yes, I'd had more than one conversation with him. Two or three of us had him join us for lunch at the Marriott Twin Bridges Hotel restaurant not far from the Pentagon. We saw no harm in that. We hardly risked spilling any national secrets since we knew none. But we thought we might learn something about Russian attitudes in the process.

What did *he* want to know? Number Two agent asked.

I didn't recall what we said during that lunch. Probably we talked about how we American reporters operated. We wrote stories from briefings and press releases and sometimes from copies of testimony in congressional committee hearings by the Secretary of Defense or other top Pentagon officials.

What I recalled as much as anything was the perplexed look the TASS man gave me when we ordered cocktails and I called for one of my favorites.

"A 'Black Russian'?" he asked, arching a brow.

It did not occur to me that ordering the vodka and Kahlua drink might strike a Russian as odd or perhaps full of hidden meaning. I explained that I often drank a Black Russian with a cup of black coffee for a strong caffeine jolt to perk me up after a meal or to keep me alert during a night of poker. Our TASS man watched closely as if to see whether I actually drank what I said I enjoyed.

"What did you tell him?" Number Two said, coming again with his stern style of interrogation about what the Russian might have been seeking. I said that I, as any reporter might, read carefully what Pentagon people said when testifying in congressional hearings on the Hill about Vietnam and other military matters. Executive sessions often followed the open portion of the hearings; transcripts of what was said later behind closed doors would eventually be published after being censored of top-secret material. By studying such transcripts later, I often gleaned nuggets of information that produced printworthy stories. I said I had no idea that my divulging such an ingenious information-gathering technique might put me in the crosshairs of the FBI. Neither Agent Whitehead nor Mr. Personality accompanying him seemed to appreciate my sarcasm.

A rookie reporter should learn early on that the only dumb question is the question not asked. On that occasion I was in the dumb mode. I should have asked my FBI friends what had prompted them to come quizzing me about the TASS correspondent. I don't think the two agents had sought out any other reporter. Had they tapped my phone? It would be divulged later that the government had tapped the phone of the *Boston Globe*'s Bill Beecher. The FBI obviously had been monitoring the TASS man's activities. Had they observed our lunching at the Marriott? Aha! Could it have been that our waiter was an undercover agent? I failed to get the answers I could have sought. Nor, I suspect, did J. Edgar Hoover's dynamic duo get the answers they had been seeking. We parted ways on what seemed to be a cordial basis. I never heard again from the FBI.

The briefings that occasionally brought the Russian to the Pentagon were one of several ways news originates in Washington. Press releases, news conferences, and interviews were the primary news generators. There were also backgrounders, which were private sessions usually arranged by or for a limited group of reporters. At backgrounders some high-ranking person or knowledgeable insider would talk on condition that he or she not be identified by name but referred to by some vague label, such as "defense officials" or "State Department sources." A good reporter developed good sources of his own. The effort paid off in good stories.

Robert Strange McNamara was Secretary of Defense for seven years and almost all the Vietnam War era of the 1960s and 1970s. He occasionally held backgrounders for select reporters known to focus on covering the Pentagon. McNamara was allowed to be identified as "US officials." Such anonymity presumably left him freer to air his views about Vietnam issues, although he was loathe to ever suggest that the war was a mistake or being conducted the wrong way. Still, whenever a spate of news stories broke simultaneously quoting "US officials" about Vietnam, it was pretty much an open secret in Washington who was doing the talking.

Leaks of juicy information were commonplace. Politics is a rough

THE ASSOCIATED PRESS
50 ROCKEFELLER PLAZA
NEW YORK, N. Y. 10020

December 22, 1969.

Chief of Bureau Arrowsmith,
Washington.

Dear Marv:

Congratulations to Bob Horton for his advance word last Monday that the new Nixon troop pullout figure would be 50,000. Bob was, as you know, right on the nose and hours ahead of the televised announcement.

Sincerely yours,

Lou

LOUIS D. BOCCARDI
MANAGING EDITOR

A note of praise from AP headquarters in New York.

game, and well-timed driblets of information or gossip can serve to advance some individual or party agenda, or undercut that of an adversary. A savvy reporter who becomes the recipient of a leak has to be aware that he possibly is being used as a tool for someone's devious purpose. Or a leak might be a case of an official's seeking to curry favor with a reporter; it might even be merely an act of friendship because of a working or social relationship.

One day a young Army officer who worked in the Pentagon's information office across the hall from the press room stopped by my desk a few minutes before noon. He said he knew of a good story. I'm listening. Would I agree to delay one hour before putting it on the wire to give him time to leave the building so as not to be suspected of having leaked it to me? Tell me more.

He motioned for me to follow him at a discreet distance. He led me into a men's room down the hall. Checking first to see that the stalls were unoccupied, he proceeded to tell me in hushed tones that an official press release was set to be released later in the day: A controversial new fighter-bomber promoted by McNamara had crashed in Thailand. I immediately saw the potential significance in what might otherwise have been interesting but not necessarily front-page news. The loss of the F-111 aircraft was likely to make the secretary of defense look bad because it could validate complaints by the generals and admirals that his insistence on making weapons cost-effective caused military capabilities to suffer.

Originally developed as the TFX, the F-111 had been flown secretly to the war zone for a test of its revolutionary variable-sweep wing and a new radar that guided the plane in flight by following the terrain. The Air Force argued from the start that McNamara's design would lack the tactical fighter capabilities it wanted, and the Navy couldn't see the big plane as being the best attack aircraft for operating off carriers. McNamara's "cost-effective" drive had become a bitter pill for the traditionally free-spending services to swallow.

My story soon burst onto the wire labeled *URGENT* and within hours was being displayed prominently on the front page of the early afternoon edition of the *Washington Star*. A civilian information official from across the hall came rushing to my desk in the press room, practically wringing his hands over the fact that I had sent out a story they weren't ready to release. I shrugged. Stuff happens.

Why had an Army information officer leaked the story to me? The answer had nothing to do with anti-McNamara animosities or interservice rivalries. We simply happened to be buddies who sat in on Friday night poker games in homes around the Virginia and Maryland suburbs.

The most consistent way of having a story widely used—and getting ego-boosting mention in the weekly AP log—was to redo or update a morning story for the next evening cycle with its fourteen hundred or so member newspapers. This became after-hours routine for me. Sherry would be washing dishes and the boys left alone with TV or homework while I isolated myself with a tall glass of bourbon to pencil out a rough draft of a story. Sometimes the boys were asleep by the time I finished dictating the piece to the office. The work-at-home routine did not qualify as quality time with the family. It was my way of trying to show my stuff in the early years in Washington.

THE SECRETARY OF DEFENSE
WASHINGTON

December 18, 1969

Dear Bob:

The gift that cheers is always a welcome one and I thank you very much for adding to my Christmas spirit.

I am delighted that you received the cheese in good order and that the little touch of Wisconsin meets with your approval.

Your thoughtfulness is really appreciated and I hope that you, too, will have a Merry Christmas and Happy New Year.

Sincerely,

Mel

Mr. Robert Horton
The Associated Press
1300 Connecticut Avenue, N.W.
Washington, D.C. 20036

Thanks for dropping by tonight
Merry Christmas
Mel Laird

Secretary of State Melvin Laird delivered a holiday gift of cheese to a Pentagon reporter who reciprocated with a bottle of wine.

The award from the Associated Press Managing Editors and the extra effort I put into the job was paying off. My paycheck was boosted by about a third, which helped Sherry and me to buy a five-bedroom home in Vienna, Virginia, a cozy little town some seventeen miles from Washington. It was our good fortune that the owner was an Air Force officer who wanted to sell the house right away to report for a second tour of duty in Southeast Asia; his willingness to hold an IOU from me for five thousand dollars made the house deal possible.

We moved into our Vienna split-level in mid-1969, and soon I was taking the family to the beach for a week at Ocean City, Maryland. The Atlantic was a chill steely gray, the sun was bright and salty, and Bob Dylan sounded in a post-protest mood, singing a ballad called "Lay Lady Lay." The good life was ours for the taking.

9

Buying a five-bedroom split-level in a fairly affluent Virginia neighborhood wasn't as simple as signing a five-thousand-dollar IOU on the side. To pull off the transaction I also bled our checking account of its few hundred dollars and borrowed fifteen hundred from a local small-loan office. Triplet payments on a mortgage, a consumer loan, and the personal paper held by our Air Force friend created an ongoing budgetary bind for the Horton household. That's what eventually brought a long, black limousine to pick me up at the Potomac River entrance to the Pentagon on a fine spring day in 1970.

The limousine was the personal vehicle of the postmaster general of the United States. He wasn't in it. One Robert Stevenson had sent a driver to chauffeur me across the Potomac to headquarters of the US Post Office Department downtown. Stevenson had been on the AP's world desk when I first arrived in Washington. He was urging me to join him on the information staff of the PMG, as they referred to the head mailman, and the prospect of earning five thousand dollars more a year than the AP was paying me was alluring. Being escorted into the city by limousine was a persuasive tactic. It gave a man a feeling of prominence.

For a reporter to desert to the enemy side and become a government mouthpiece is generally scorned by his peers. But for many months a sense of ego had compelled me to do extra work after-hours for the grand old AP; going to work for the government would relieve me of that self-imposed burden. And so I jumped.

I was hardly the first to nibble at the opportunity to bring home a fatter paycheck working for the government. Three other former newsmen were among the half-dozen people in the PMG's public information office. The staff was headed by a former UPI man, Jim Holland, who had the imposing title of assistant postmaster general for public affairs. His deputy was Bob Stevenson, who'd sent the limo across the Potomac to lure me from the Pentagon. News editor Jamie Cain was a reporter out of South Carolina. Hank Lewis came from the old *Washington Times Herald* with an interesting tale; he had supervised the early journalistic career as an "enquiring photographer" of a young Jacqueline Bouvier, who had become known later as First Lady Jackie Kennedy. The US Post Office Department had no female information officers, but each man had a female secretary to type out his press releases and other copy on the latest correction-capable Selectric typewriters. That struck me as a nice side benefit for someone who for years himself had hammered away at manual typewriters.

We all were cloistered in the US Post Office's massive headquarters building at 12th and Pennsylvania Avenue. It was built in 1899, four decades before I was born. Despite being one of the most imposing downtown structures in its day—as it still is—the building was really no architectural beauty. Romanesque arches on low, clustered columns made it look like "a cross between a cathedral and a cotton mill," as the *New York Times* once described it. At the top was a soaring bell tower one might expect to periodically disgorge hordes of bats. Before the building was even ten years old people were demanding that it be demolished.

Why the postal system needed a platoon of people to deal with the press was a reasonable question. Surely there weren't that many inquiries coming in from stamp collectors. Was it because people called in demanding to know why the price of a stamp had jumped from three cents in the early 1950s to eight cents in the early '70s? Bigger stuff than that, Bob Stevenson told me. If the right strings were pulled in Congress, the Post Office Department would be morphing into a corporatelike and supposedly more efficient US Postal Service. The o utlook was good because of widespread recognition that the old way of having Congress appoint postmasters based on their political connections instead of their business know-how had kept the system in continual need of millions of dollars in subsidies. Information officers would play a key role in explaining to Americans the importance of Congress's passing the necessary postal reform legislation to create the new US Postal Service.

The "bigger stuff" going on in Congress wasn't what swayed me to accept the job. There were other attractions. Being chauffeured into town in a limo had given me an illusory feeling of importance. A smooth operator was my ol' buddy Bob Stevenson, but that limo ride would be the one and only time I'd ever sit in the PMG's shiny black car. The prospect of having a secretary, ideally like a trim blonde I'd seen down the hall, also was interesting; no one told me that my secretary would be a plump Jewish grandmother who seemed to think her job description included constantly chattering about her personal life.

The bigger paycheck swung the deal. Initially I would be put on the payroll as a government "consultant" at the rate of $125 a day, double my earnings with the wire service. Getting the appropriate Civil Service rating—a high-ranking GS15—would take a few weeks. I'd heard that the screening process had all sorts of complications and uncertainties. Jamie Cain, the news chief who had been in the government for years, blew that off. No, he said, smiling, they knew how to get a prospective employee's paperwork shuffled to the top of the usual pyramid of applications from other job seekers.

Our compatriot Hank Lewis had a seat on a government committee whose members from other departments, such as Commerce and Treasury, culled through applications until settling on their respective choices for new hires. A wink and a nudge got the job done to the satisfaction of each agency. *You agree to the man I want for my department, I'll agree to yours.*

I had been on board a few months when Congress passed the Postal Reorganization Act creating the new US Postal Service; President Richard Nixon signed it into law on August 12, 1970. The White House gave us souvenir pens bearing a replica of the president's signature. We were told they were used in Nixon's signing of the historic legislation abolishing the old cabinet-level Post Office Department. I had my doubts, but the assertion made us feel important.

By then I had a work routine that was really humdrum compared with the high-octane news activity I knew at the Pentagon. I drafted press releases now and then, answered calls from reporters asking for

THE POSTMASTER GENERAL
WASHINGTON, D. C. 20260

September 15, 1970

Dear Bob:

Together with President Nixon, I am pleased to send you this personal memento from the historic signing ceremony here at the Department on August 12, 1970 which enacted the Postal Reorganization Act (P.L. 91-375) into law.

With kind regards.

Sincerely,

Winton M. Blount

Mr. Bob Horton
Public Information Officer
Room 3346
Post Office Department
Washington, D. C. 20260

Postmaster General Winton Blount's presentation of a pen used by President Richard M. Nixon to sign the Postal Reorganization Act of 1970.

details about how the new USPS would operate, and even filled requests from the public for postal pamphlets. Writing press releases was no challenge after years of reading handouts from government agencies. I knew intuitively the format, but I had little enthusiasm for the content. A press release about Smalltown, USA, getting a new post office wasn't quite as attention grabbing as a Pentagon report on Vietnam casualties or an umpteen-million-dollar contract for building a new warplane.

The highest priority of the news office day in and day out became lunching at the Crown Restaurant, which was frequented mainly by government employees downtown. Our postal party usually consisted of Bob Stevenson, Jamie Cain, and me, along with Don Campbell, who for years had been an advance man making travel arrangements for PMGs touring post offices around the country. This was a daytime cocktail crowd unlike any I'd ever known; ordering three drinks seemed to be the usual minimum. Jamie and Don had their bourbons, and I'd have three or four Martinis, but Bob Stevenson was the iron man among us. He typically had three vodka Gibsons before the food arrived and would follow those with a couple of bottles of ale. Bob was truly the kind of supervisor a drinking man could appreciate. With the size of tabs we ran up, the proprietor tried his best to have a table available to us as soon as we stepped in the door.

Leaving at five in the afternoon meant braving heavy traffic heading out the George Washington Parkway for the half-hour drive to home in Vienna. Delaying to let traffic clear out was a good excuse to linger downtown for a happy hour or two, as others often did. Doing so often made me late for the nice dinners that Sherry had diligently prepared for us all. Sometimes the wife and I would be at the table alone, Bobby and Doug having eaten and gone to their rooms or to the den for TV. We didn't talk that much. Sherry surely had no interest in hearing what silly questions I'd gotten from reporters about postal matters. She said little about how her day had gone, possibly because I seldom asked. She was a wife who accepted my late arrivals with great patience. At least I wouldn't be spending the rest of the evening sipping a drink and working late on an AP rewrite. I sometimes did have one or two as she cleaned the kitchen alone.

10

An odyssey to Mexico was supposed to have been one of the idyllic times of our marriage. It did not turn out to be so. The journey began with tears and ended with tears.

The first tears came after our plane descended to Mexico City, deep into a lake of smog. The downtown area lay submerged under what appeared to be smoke, as if the entire city were on fire. The air had a stinging acidity that kept us mopping our eyes as we taxied to the hotel. It would have been less painful facing the gusts of a West Texas dust storm.

What we knew about our eventual destination was only what I'd culled from travel magazines. San Miguel de Allende, a historic village that had been found by a Franciscan monk in the 1500s, had become a nesting place of writers, painters, and expatriate US retirees. Sherry didn't object when I suggested we go there in the summer of 1972. She probably felt that it would be good to get away to ourselves and rebond. I had a fanciful notion that we might eventually settle there to live cheaply and perhaps happily ever after. We'd leave our sons with relatives in Texas for the week; the boys and their grandparents would enjoy that. Sherry and I would be joined in San Miguel by our longtime Lubbock friends Everett and Katy Groseclose, who had moved to New Jersey to be near Everett's new *Wall Street Journal* assignment in New York.

We stayed overnight in a hotel in Mexico City in the *zona rosa*, which wasn't a red light district but rather, we were told, a trendy "pink zone" where many Americans lodged. There were shops and dance clubs (strip joints, too), taxi drivers hawking tours, and an unending cacophony of automobile horns. The streets were a gauntlet of pleas and sometimes outright demands for money from beggars, some of whom made it a profitable profession. I saw one pathetic, soot-faced hag, hunkered against a building, accept a dollar from a tourist and wrap it around a roll of paper bills fat enough to choke Pancho Villa's horse.

My decision to save a few pesos put us on what may have been the cheapest, dingiest, most crowded bus to San Miguel. If any other passengers spoke English, they didn't bother using it on us, not that we could have been unnoticed as Americans. We were the quiet ones whose apparel—my ocean blue polyester trousers and Sherry's pink polished cotton slacks—practically screamed *touristas*. It should not have been a surprise if a failure to communicate had sent us out on the wrong bus.

As our four-hour ride north progressed, so did the feeling that I had made a horrible choice about where I was leading not only us but also our friends from New Jersey. The terrain was barely a cut above barren desert: hot, dry, sparsely grassed, and, I could imagine, infested with deadly scorpions and creeping Gila monsters. Lord, I was thinking, don't let this rattletrap break down out here.

Soon to my relief the bus topped a rise and began taking us down a gentle slope toward an astonishingly picturesque village. Stretched out below us was a scene no postcard could have done justice to. A multi-spired church towered above leafy plazas and shops that I had read dated back to the seventeenth and eighteenth centuries. Catching a glimpse of a burro pulling a two-wheeled wooden wagon down a cobbled street gave me a sense of relief about the soundness of my vacation recommendation.

Doing in Mexico as Mexicans are said to do meant to me locating a pleasant little cantina as soon as possible. We'd do that after checking into the Instituto Allende. My pretrip research advised me that the arts and culture center offered clean, comfortable beds, with a restaurant and a bar. While Sherry freshened herself in the room, I slipped away for a quick cerveza to invigorate me for the stroll downtown.

A sweet allure of flowers kept us wandering in the main *jardin* before we located a cantina. That was all right. I had one cerveza under my belt. Sherry read San Miguel history from a pamphlet while I became mesmerized staring at the high reaches of La Parroquia, a church built in the seventeenth century with many spires and topped with a great white cross. Its ornate neogothic visage stood in stark relief against the hard blue sky, and suddenly I was swept with one of those odd sensations of déjà vu. It was as if I had stood in that exact spot at another time, experiencing the same awesome expanse of heaven and feeling an identical sense of spirituality about it all. Or, I wondered later, was it that I'd simply seen a similarity between La Parroquia and the Spanish-tiled administration building at Texas Tech with its big bell tower?

The cantina we came across was not a stylish place with the kind of gay ambiance that I'm sure Sherry would have preferred. In the dim lighting the tables and chairs with their scars and other evidence of hard use might have seemed vintage residue of another century but likely were hundred-proof contemporary throw-away stuff. No mariachi band played, and there was no neon sign on the wall promoting a particular cerveza. But the waiter came promptly, grinning as he wiped his hands on his apron. He promptly brought our Carta Blancas, first one for each of us, then a second for me. I soon inquired about the mezcal, a liquor made from the same plant as tequila, but Sherry somehow knew that I was angling to switch to harder stuff than the beer and gave me a severe look that said please don't start that now. I compromised by settling for a third Carta Blanca, but the moment of carefree kicking back and enjoying the good life had taken a blow.

Montezuma's revenge delivered the next blow. Enjoying the good life over a previous night's plate of creamy enchiladas would not come without penalty, and I began to suffer severe stomach cramps early the first evening in San Miguel. By midnight I was feverish, reeling with delirium and wishing I could die, but not on a bathroom throne. Dawn found me too shaky from loss of water to be thinking of alcohol. Sherry quietly nursed me back to an ability to stand and finally walk about.

The arrival of our friends the Grosecloses helped revive me. Sherry's mood improved. We chatted exuberantly, laughing and talking about times when we were reporters running around covering convenience store holdups, beauty pageants, and bad car wrecks for the *Lubbock Avalanche-Journal*. I tried not to disturb the mood of the moment, but soon I was reflecting in a melancholy way about the different directions our careers had taken after leaving Texas Tech. Everett had to serve a tour of duty in the Army shortly after I left the *A-J* to join the AP in Tennessee. He'd later gotten on with the *Wall Street Journal* and showed every intention of making a career of it. I, on the other hand, had exchanged a challenging and exciting assignment as a Washington correspondent for the humdrum routine of a government flack. I began to realize how much I missed being a reporter. I began to realize, too, how improbable if not impossible it would be ever to turn back.

I don't remember drinking too much. Lack of memory may be a tip-off that in fact I did. I do recall a sharp argument with Sherry in our room after we'd all been out and about, browsing shops and, with some urging by me, stopping in at whatever next cantina came in sight. I know that at some point I passed up the cerveza to test the mezcal and that Sherry thought drinking that atop beer was not a wise thing. She became upset. But I thought, hey, this was supposed to be about fun and adventure in Mexico. This was all about the good life.

Tears that began with the smog in Mexico City returned for yet another reason in San Miguel. On the day before we were to return to Mexico City for our flight back to Lubbock, the hotel clerk handed me a message saying I should call home. I sensed that such a message could only mean bad news; I was hoping that it didn't involve one of our sons. As it turned out, Bobby and Doug were all right, but—. Grandad Horton had died of a stroke. Because the family had difficulty locating us in Mexico, funeral arrangements could not be delayed. Sherry and I would not make it back in time for the service in the little Methodist Church at Meadow.

Grandad Horton was one of the kindest, most gentle-spirited men I have ever known, next only to my own father. Being unable to be at his funeral added to the sense of loss. I was normally quite good at stuffing my emotions. Not this time. This was one occasion when emotions would not be suppressed.

11

We had planned to linger in Lubbock only a day or two following the trip to Mexico, but I wasn't about to return to Washington without visiting Grandad Horton's grave. It would be a moment to revive memories of how he had lived and what his life had meant to me. It would also be a time to reflect on what Bob Horton should be doing with the remainder of his life.

A two-lane blacktop extends from the edge of Meadow, Texas, going a half-mile west before curving a half-mile north to a higher elevation of cropland. There, surrounded by fields of cotton, is the New Meadow Cemetery. "New" probably was once a justifiable descriptive, but by 1972 the cemetery had been receiving the remains of departed souls for more than half a century. I strolled among the white monuments and bronze markers before finally spotting freshly turned soil of the latest burial site. A broad bronze marker bore the name of Belle Horton, my grandmother, who had died in 1968. The name Bert C. Horton was not yet stamped onto the plate.

Interesting what one will remember while pausing at a grave. Grandad rocked me to sleep in his lap when I was about three years old and my parents were off somewhere. How comforting it felt snuggling against his chest as he hummed a little song, which he often did as he went about during the day. Grandad was a happy man. He was happy having a grandson in his lap. I'd be peering up at the old boxlike wooden clock on the living room wall. Its pendulum swung back and forth, almost in time with Grandad's humming, clicking away the time as we rocked.

Something always stood out as instructive to me about Grandad's character. When he was a young farmer life handed him a setback painful enough that other men might have dived headlong into the bottle. In 1920 he'd moved the family from Texas to farm in Arizona. Cotton prices had soared during World War I. The outlook was good, but when the Great War ended in 1918, Europeans returned to farming, and the eventual loss of overseas markets sent US farm prices plunging. In the spring of 1920 cotton was bringing forty cents a pound. By December the price had fallen to fourteen cents, and Grandad saw that he couldn't eke out a living. He sold what he had to buy a car and hurry back to Texas.

My brother Joe interviewed Grandad before he died and asked him whether he hadn't liked Arizona. Grandad smiled. What he didn't like was having lost almost everything. They'd owned a ten-acre plot at Scottsdale. No telling what that land would have become worth in years to come. "One time I could've made five thousand dollars," Grandad said. "Real estate man came out there and wanted it and we decided, well, we could get that crop and sell the land for that and that thing [the cotton market] went down and we didn't get anything. I lost six thousand dollars." My grandfather was thirty-three when he was forced to start over with little more than his two hands and a determination not to give up. He built a shack for the family to live in on a quarter-section of unbroken land north of Meadow, cleared it of mesquite and grass, and once again began planting cotton. Twenty years of hard work later, he was rocking a little grandson in a bigger, cozier home on a piece of fertile farmland that was just about paid for. Grandad Horton earned his opportunity to hum happily.

Something in the recollections at his gravesite set me to thinking. I needed to reconsider a few things I'd been pondering about my own life. Bob Dylan said the answer was blowing in the wind. What was it telling me? I was thirty-three, the same age as my grandfather had been when he was forced to retreat and restart a life, but I had lost nothing compared with what life had taken from him. Of my own free will I had walked away from one career that had seemed to have some relevance, opting for another that held little meaning for me, and merely a bit more money. I might have been making another questionable decision if I dragged the family to Mexico with the fanciful notion that I'd write great novels while living an easy tequila life in the hot desert sun. What about my wife, my two sons? What kind of life would that be for them?

Another grave bore the Horton name. Off in a less-tended plot of sparse grass was a foot-high, trapezoid-shaped marker with the inscription Sammie Keith Horton, March 15, 1947. My mother's third son, after Joe Bert and me, had died within hours of being delivered in the hospital at Brownfield. Choking on or choked by something seemed to have been the cause, although it was never quite clear to us.

At the time of that tragedy we lived in the Union community south of Brownfield, in Terry County, where grasslands in the 1940s were still being plowed into farm fields. Mama began having contractions and was taken to the hospital on that March morning in 1947, and I was left playing with the Kennedy girls in their farmhouse near Meadow. One of my mother's sisters came in the door that afternoon saying "Sis's baby died!" We were crouched on the floor playing jacks, my aunt Peggy, only two months older than I, and my aunt Jimmie Lee, who was just a year older. I suppose death is of little significance to children playing games. After hearing the news we just went back to bouncing the rubber ball, sweeping the jacks into hands cupped against the floor, Pigs in the Pen.

The loss of a child was a stark lesson for Mama a year later when her next newborn had a brush with death. She was busying herself around the farmhouse at Union, maybe sewing or washing dishes, while my new little sis Linda Faye was asleep on our parents' bed in a room off the kitchen. Linda somehow toppled from the bed, striking her head hard on the pinewood floor. Blood suddenly flowed from a cut above her eye. Mama grabbed her up and with a pillow case and the hem of her skirt began mopping at the wound. The blood kept coming. Crimson ran between her fingers.

With her husband off somewhere working, Mama thought no more than a few moments before deciding she needed help. *I will not lose this little girl*. Unable to staunch the blood, she hurried out the door and began running down a dirt road. The nearest house was a mile away, and running with a child clasped to her breast, she might have fallen exhausted before getting help. By God's grace a car appeared where cars seldom drove, and a Good Samaritan sped them twelve miles to Brownfield, where a doctor stitched the wound.

The route from the cemetery took me past the First Baptist Church in Meadow and through another thicket of memories of death on Mama's side of the family, the brood of her father, Joe Walter Kennedy. He was Paw-Paw to me. He and Granny Kennedy had twelve children, one of whom died in infancy. Mama was the second oldest of nine girls. That meant that I grew up, sort of, with several teenage aunts. On up the line from Peggy Joyce and Jimmie Lee, in progressively higher ages, were Georgia Lou; Sue Lane; Patsy Merle; Doris Laverne; Velma Lee; my mother, Viola Faye; and the oldest, Omagene. They were chatty, lively aunts, and I loved being around them. I was able to spend less time with their brothers, my uncles Billy and Buster, who were often out working in the fields. They were less talkative, probably because female voices dominated their days.

I was the princely nephew of a wonderfully happy bunch. When my parents drove us out to the Kennedy farm on the rented Hunter place south of Meadow, the girls would skip out to the car waving and laughing. They were delighted to have a boy playmate for a change. We'd play jacks and skip rope and sometimes climb trees. I thrived on the cheers of girls, then and later.

The Kennedy clan lost Granny Kennedy in 1952. She began hemorrhaging during surgery in the hospital at Brownfield, down the road from Meadow. Older than she should have been at age fifty-two, she died on the operating table.

Granny's daughters witnessed it all through the wide window of a viewing room: the bloody cloths, the frantic pace of nurses around the operating table. The fatal drama playing out beyond the glass left them with a growing sense of helplessness and despair, and then their mother was gone. Jimmie Lee, barely a teenager, angrily confronted the doctor, demanding to know how come they had killed her mother. His unsatisfactory explanation: She died because the hospital had run out of blood to replenish what the hemorrhaging had taken from her. Peggy, the youngest, blanked out the memory of those moments, never again to recall anything about her mother's dying—or even the funeral, which was one of only a few rare times I ever saw my own mother weep.

I still can hear the echoes of Paw-Paw's wailing and moaning throughout the funeral service in the First Baptist Church in Meadow. He was stricken with grief but also troubled about what lay ahead for him and the family. Sons Billy and Buster might be able to take care of themselves, but what about that gaggle of girls? Three of the oldest were married at the time. The others soon sought out young men to wed. Paw-Paw was left with his farm and his memories.

It would be years before I discovered that my parents owned eight gravesites at the New Meadow Cemetery where my infant brother Sammie Keith was laid in a tiny coffin. They obviously considered the possibility that our whole family might eventually be buried there. As it turned out, they chose their own burials at a cemetery in Lubbock. Left uncertain was who would wind up in one of the spaces next to the deceased infant. I had a notion who one might be.

12

We were the young and restless of our time, with passions no less intense than those of any who came before us or probably any to come later. We held hands between classes and went to drive-in movies to cuddle and whisper sincere words to one another. When we weren't riding shotgun in pickup trucks, we packed ourselves six or seven to a car, cruising the streets without speeding because it was about being seen, not flashing by too swiftly to be noticed. Few were the boys who didn't imagine heroic performances under Friday night lights. Few, too, the girls who didn't scheme to rush out at game's end to escort chosen heroes from the field of battle. Elvis sang, "Won't you wear my ring around your neck," and some couples went steady all the way to the altar.

Visiting the old high school before returning to Washington revived for me scenes that could have been spliced together from a PBS documentary and a brassy made-for-TV movie. It was a melange of memories reflecting influences that stitched me into the person I would become.

Digging into history, I learned that the Meadow School District was formed in 1904. At first, all grades attended classes in a wooden four-room structure. A two-story red brick building was erected in 1923. A separate high school didn't exist until 1935. I graduated there in 1957.

The high school building included a gymnasium, so it wasn't difficult for students in certain classes to hear the thud of basketballs on hardwood as teams practiced. Overlooking the court was a stage used for school plays, choruses, assemblies, and annual graduation ceremonies. A great theater curtain could be drawn across the stage to provide some privacy for rehearsals and such. But the curtain hardly insulated the stage from the sounds of coaches' whistles and grunts and shouts on the court.

Classes were out for the weekend that day I took a walk around the school grounds. When I was in school the gym often was left open for any who had an urge to shoot baskets and perhaps organize a pickup game. Wondering if that would still be the case, I grasped the knob of a rear door. Ah! It was in fact unlocked. I stepped cautiously inside to be sure no one was there and—.

In my mind the tinkling of a distant piano echoed from behind the curtain drawn across the stage facing down on the basketball court. The curtain dissolved to an old scene that played out many afternoons when Glen D Hardin and I practiced music. His piano playing accompanying my singing surely created a nuisance for the girls' team practicing for the next game. But we thought we had an important challenge coming up, too.

Ag teacher Doc Babb envisioned Glen D and me as successors to Sonny Curtis as State FFA entertainer performing at Future Farmers of America banquets that took place all across Texas in the spring. Glen D and I were sophomores when Sonny left with his guitar to finish his senior year at Slaton. Glen D had a natural talent for playing the piano by ear. We all knew that he was, as they say, destined. Some people applauded my singing.

I had always wanted to sing. At fourteen I'd be out under a windmill warbling enthusiastically for a half-dozen cockeyed chickens and a cow chewing cud just beyond a barbed-wire fence. At first I wailed the Hank Williams songs of the day. Later I mimicked the smoother, note-bending style of Lefty Frizzell, who was quite as popular as Hank in the early fifties. They paired for a tour in their early glory days in 1951, swapping the headliner spot at times. Hank played Lefty's embossed guitar when Lefty waited his turn in a suit glittering with sequins and adorned with the leather fringe of a buffalo hunter's jacket. I admired the flair as I admired the voice.

Being a Frizzell clone in the Hardin-Horton show might have been a turning point in my life, for better or worse. Perhaps worse, given my tendency to be too adventuresome. But Glen D's family also soon

Lefty Frizzell (early 1950s publicity photo).

moved from Meadow, and my fantasy of a career in country music died. Glen D went on to play professionally, ultimately even with Elvis Presley. Sonny, who would play the guitar when I sang at school or at some talent contest, performed with Buddy Holly in their teenage years and went on to be inducted into the Nashville Songwriters Hall of Fame. I set off on a different track, diverted to a career in the news business by more astute people than a few classmates who sometimes cheered my singing. I'd ponder later what might have been, but the news business was my future.

Missing from the school grounds during my wandering there in the summer of 1972 was the old two-story red brick building that once held classes for students of each age level. It was demolished in the fifties to make way for a new elementary school building and a new gymnasium where we played our basketball games, starting in 1956. Part of my first-grade year was spent in the old building in 1946. I'd begun school in Santa Fe, but we moved from New Mexico because my dad wanted to get back to farming in West Texas. Memories of those days were dim, just as I recall the halls and the classrooms themselves as being rather shadowy. I may have been mistaken about that; the school at Meadow

Sonny Curtis wrote and performed such songs as "I Fought The Law, and the Law Won," and "The Real Buddy Holly Story" (Dot Records publicity photo, 1958).

probably did have electric lights. The new Rural Electrification Administration had brought power to towns in West Texas in the late 1930s, yet farmhouses were not electrified even in the early '40s.

The way youngsters were schooled then seems pleasantly quaint. I sat at a combination chair and desk that had a hinged writing sur-

David Frizzell (right) talking about his brother Lefty at the Buddy Holly Center in Lubbock (2014).

face that could be raised to expose a shallow drawerlike box for storing soft-leaded number 2 pencils, little scissors with round-tipped blades, a box of Crayolas, and a Big Chief tablet of paper with a cover depicting an Indian in feathered headdress. Everyone had a Big Chief tablet, but I think that those quickly faded into the realm of memorabilia. They became victims of a coming political correctness.

Our teacher used long, fat sticks of chalk to scrawl letters of the alphabet on the blackboard. She'd wipe away her scrawlings at the close of class with a felt eraser that often sent a puff of white dust into the air, depending on how hard she slapped the eraser against the blackboard. If she'd somehow been perturbed by the way class had gone, the sound of the eraser popping the black surface would be loud enough to make a kid jump. That may have been her intention.

A yellow school bus picked me up on a rough dirt road about fifty yards from the farmhouse that my dad rented for us several miles out from Meadow. A stretch of sandy field lay between the house and the road, and that has served a good purpose for me. My mother made me wear suspenders, probably because my pants didn't fit me snugly. I hated those suspenders, because no one else wore them and they made me feel sissified. Upon leaving home in the morning I'd unsnap the elastic straps and stuff them in my pocket as soon as the house and Mama were out of sight. When the bus dropped me off in the afternoon, I would lie down in a sandy furrow and reattach them to my britches as best I could, hoping Mama wasn't watching from the window. I think she must have seen and must have understood, because soon she stopped making me wear the silly things. I myself had no continuous years of schooling at Meadow. We moved to nearby Brownfield for a while, then I was in the third grade at Odessa, and from the fourth grade into my eighth-grade year I was schooled in the Union community in southern Terry County. I reentered school at Meadow midway of the eighth grade. and that's where I finished those intoxicating glory days of high school.

How they could be intoxicating, literally, began in 1956. My initial experience with alcohol remains just about as vividly in my mind as the feeling of one's first sexual experience. I was sixteen, riding in the back seat of a '51 Chevy on Highway 82 across the New Mexico desert when I took that first drink. A high school buddy with two other pals from Meadow had driven into Cloudcroft hoping that I would join them on a jaunt south of the border. They'd been to Juarez and planned to cross the line again to sample a few more slow gin fizzes at a certain cantina. Never having had a droplet of booze, and always wanting to fit in with the older boys, I was willing. I didn't have a clue what a slow gin fizz was. They said the name of the drink told you what it did: hits you slow. *Oh*. One day I would learn that "slow" wasn't what I thought it was. *Slow* was really *sloe*, the small plum berry used to flavor the gin. The drinking game was a mystery to me. I had much to learn about it.

My parents and I were staying in one of several rustic rental cabins owned by my Aunt Velma at Cloudcroft in the Sacramento Mountains.

I made up an excuse that the Meadow threesome had come to take us to a movie in Alamogordo, forty miles distant. I told them that because I was sure Mama and Daddy would not cotton to my being exposed to the nightlife of Juarez, more than two hours away. Juarez had this reputation, you see. The movie excuse worked, and Daddy let me head off with three dollars. He undoubtedly felt confident that three bucks was more than enough to cover the price of a movie ticket in Alamogordo.

Chevy-drivin' Don was a senior. I was only into my sophomore year, but, having lettered as a freshman on the Meadow Broncos football team, I felt rough and ready. I'd been exposed to Elvis. I was nothing if not a true hound dog—*Let's shag!* In the fifties whenever we'd be anxious to move on to some other place or situation, we had this routine of exclaiming in unison, *Let's shag!* We wouldn't know for a long time that it meant something ribald in London. But on an amber afternoon in New Mexico, I was ready to shag.

In the fifties cars had their tanks filled with gasoline at what were called, quite sensibly, filling stations. People could also fill up with a supply of alcoholic beverages if a liquor store happened to be nearby. When my driver Don stopped along the way, a liquor store did just happen to be a few steps away from the gasoline pumps, the kind with tall glass tanks above the hoses so that you could see the fuel bubbling down as an attendant was filling the car. The three dollars my dad had given me paid for a pint of red wine with change left over. As soon as Don's Chevy peeled away, I broke the metal cap of the bottle and with a certain anticipation began taking the first sips of the young, wild life.

And so I waited. When would I be feeling it, I wondered? I kept waiting, and my three pals kept looking at me, grinning, until after a few minutes I learned how it did feel. *Different*.

Something about the world changed the instant the alcohol in my blood hit my brain. Things become extremely pleasant. Any uneasiness or guilt that I might have had faded like the setting sun. I glanced out the window and saw Burma Shave signs and other desert things streaming by in slow motion, even with the needle displayed in the Chevy's speedometer leaning past eighty miles per hour.

Had I known before that drive down a New Mexico mountain what the sensation of alcohol would be, I'd have cracked a bottle much sooner.

Had I had known the consequences of chasing that sensation throughout later years, I might have remained in the car at that filling station and not set foot in the liquor store next door. You often hear people say that had they known then what they would know later, they would have behaved a lot differently. That is indeed what they say. But who knows?

13

Nineteen-seventy-two became a tumultuous year for the nation. I wasn't feeling so wonderful about things myself. In October of 1972 President Richard Nixon's effort to oust a special prosecutor assigned to investigate sleazy political activities set off a chain of events that would force him from office. Someone had broken into Democratic National Committee offices in the Watergate apartment complex in Washington attempting to learn details of the political strategy the Democrats might be using in opposing Nixon's reelection. Had Nixon himself ordered the break-in? When the special prosecutor sought tape recordings of conversations in the White House, Nixon demanded that the Justice Department fire him. Two top Justice Department officials resigned in tandem rather than do Nixon's bidding. A third complied, and the special prosecutor was gone. In an ensuing firestorm of public criticism, Congress turned Sherlock Holmes. Threatened with impeachment, Nixon eventually had to resign.

I didn't have tumult on a scale as grand as Nixon's, but enough had happened to leave me disillusioned with life, or really with myself. I had left a nice news career to take a humdrum government job for more money and felt restive about what I was doing. I drank heavily. I was secretive about activities affecting my marriage and blind to where all that might lead. What should have been the best of times was becoming the worst of times.

The unfolding of the Watergate drama on television had an impact on me. Television provided live coverage of congressional hearings that focused on what the president knew, and when, about the break-in. I envied seeing former cohorts of mine at work with their pens, pads, and hand-held recorders. I suddenly realized how much I missed the news business.

The catalyst for a personal resolve to get back to where I had been came with news of Nixon's dismissal of the two top Justice Department officials on October 21, 1972. Sherry and I happened to be in a Dallas hotel room on a trip with some of her former classmates to see the Cowboys play the Giants. When a White House reporter breathlessly reported news of Nixon's "Saturday Night Massacre," I became so angry I took off a shoe and threw it at the television set. Drinking helped trigger the outburst, but I was not alone in feeling outrage. The White House was quickly besieged with complaints from citizens throughout the nation about what they considered to be an arrogant abuse of presidential power.

With such historic activity going on in Washington, how could one not want to be back in the game? I suspected that landing a decent news job after being sidelined for three years might be difficult, but I had no idea how really involved and painful the effort would be. For too long I was like a dog chasing its tail.

After our journey to Mexico, Sherry and I were back in Virginia needing new beginnings in marriage and career. I know she tried desperately to find a solution for dealing with a husband unable to get his priorities straight. I was putting self-satisfaction and personal ambition before family. I could not or would not see that I was the problem. There came a day when we sat across from each other in our living room in Vienna, saying little, not really knowing what to say or how. At Sherry's suggestion we had found a marriage counselor and attended a few sessions, sometimes together, sometimes separately. The solution that finally evolved—ours, not the counselor's—was to leave Washington and return to Texas. The idea of seeking a new life in Mexico was not realistic, but that option would always be there after we settled at least for a time in Lubbock.

In the summer of 1972 we found a new home in Lubbock that came with an abandoned young border collie that our two sons couldn't bear to send away. Over my objection we kept the pup, naming him Freddie the Freeloader. The mooching little pooch was to become a member of the family for years. Our eldest son, Bobby, began his freshman year at the new Coronado High School. Doug enrolled in Wheelock Elementary just up the street from our house on Chicago Avenue. Sherry, as always, was the dedicated, fastidious homemaker. I joined with my father in housing construction. He had already built several homes around Lubbock. He printed up a card announcing the new partnership of R. W. Horton and Son.

Dad bought three lots outside Lubbock at Ransom Canyon, which had a lake fringed by a scattering of homes, some quite expensive, others only modest vacation dwellings. We built one of the first houses on the canyon rim overlooking the water. It was an enjoyable time in a different form of work. Occasionally, however, out on the job, sweating in the summer sun, a self-pitying thought would rag at me, an imagined headline in the local newspaper: "Former Washington Correspondent Wields Hammer As Apprentice Carpenter."

Nevertheless, those weeks spent working with my dad—sawing, hammering, grabbing barbecue sandwiches for lunch at Pinkie's liquor store—became treasured memories. Although he had dropped out of high school as a freshman, I saw genius in the way he worked. He'd sit down at a table and unroll a house plan, anchoring its curled-up edges with an ashtray and a cup of coffee. Then he'd begin envisioning what he should start doing first out at the job site. Two hours and a half-dozen cigarettes later he'd roll up that floor plan, toss it bound with a rubber band behind the seat of his little red Toyota pickup, then go out and proceed to build a house from memory.

Even before we finished our first house for sale I was secretly mulling plans to head East. The timing of my final decision caught everyone by surprise. I did not inform my parents until the night before leaving, and it was an emotional moment. They said little and made no attempt to dissuade me, but I'm sure they were concerned to see me in such turmoil. Explaining why I felt I had to leave was more difficult than the leaving itself. Sherry was in tears during the night.

The next morning I kissed the boys goodbye before they could be fully awake. Outside in the darkness I'd loaded a Dodge van with clothes, books, stereo equipment, and my favorite records. The sun was breaking the horizon as I reached the outskirts of Lubbock, leaving behind people whose importance in my life I would not fully grasp for months to come.

By the next midnight I was turning the van into a sprawling truck stop somewhere across the Mississippi into Tennessee. I'd left space between belongings in the rear to be able to curl up for a nap. There was too much on my mind to rest easily. After sleeping less than two hours, I decided to push on, sipping from a supersized cup of coffee and keeping the radio blaring to help me stay alert.

In the early morning hours WSM radio in Nashville began talking about a new record album about to come out by Lefty Frizzell. My ears perked up. My boyhood singing idol had become an icon in country music; the new album was even titled, "The Legendary Lefty Frizzell." But his career had gone south, suffering partly because rock and roll was all but killing off country music but also because Lefty had become a sad alcoholic He had been ripped off by a manager. His records were not being promoted as he felt they should. When Columbia dropped him as a recording artist, another label hoped to capitalize on a Frizzell comeback. One song was his best in years. WSM played it. I loved it. "That's the Way Love Goes" became a number one hit when Merle Haggard recorded it. Lefty's song brought Merle his one and only Grammy.

The resurgence of an old country singer somehow had special meaning for one radio listener speeding along a highway in the dead of night, with no direction home, as Bob Dylan might have put it. My man Lefty, *on the rebound*, I was thinking. Buying a copy of that new melody for myself seemed at the moment more important than getting a new job. I still did not have my priorities straight.

14

Hands across the water hoisted me from the ranks of the unemployed. In early 1973 the British gave me the kind of job I'd been hoping to find. *God save the Queen!*

I was familiar with Reuters as a foreign news agency used by a handful of major US papers. The Brits had correspondents in more than a hundred nations, but when I was with the AP we never considered them as being anything like a competitor in this country. By the time I arrived on the scene, they were expanding operations in the United States.

Having wire service experience certainly was a key in my getting on board with Reuters. No less important was the fact that a former coworker and friend of mine in the AP bureau on Connecticut Avenue was now a Reuters man. Tom Stewart, who covered the Justice Department, had alerted me about a forthcoming opening on the Reuters staff. Charmayne Marsh was leaving to work for Speaker of the House Jim Wright of Fort Worth. I knew I could count on Tom to put in a word for me, and bless his pea-pickin' heart, it must have been a really good word. I was on the Reuters payroll right away.

The British style of journalism differed in some ways, mostly minor, from the way I had functioned as an AP reporter. For one thing, they spelled some things differently, throwing a *u* into such words as color, humor, and rumor, making them colour, humour and rumour. In the milieu of reportage on politics, war, and diplomatic affairs, I never wrote about automotive things. But had it been the case with Reuters, I learned that the fenders of cars would be called wings. The hood over

Typical press credentials.

the motor was the bonnet. If the car had a flat, one needed to find a place to fix the tyre.

Reuters' attitude toward the general handling of the news differed from the American way, at least in the manner AP and UPI men were accustomed to operating. Reuters didn't feel under competitive pressure to issue breathless bulletins or stories labeled *urgent*, items often sent zipped out a sentence at a time and sometimes with errors made in haste. The emphasis was on providing editors with a complete-package story with relevant background detail rather than rushing out a series of bulletins and urgent add-on paragraphs that required being stitched together later by local newspaper editors.

Reuters folk with their clipped, somewhat singsong kind of accent reacted with amusement hearing my twangy Texas way of talking. I felt like a gallumphing wheel of a Conestoga wagon pursued by Indians in one of those old western shoot-'em-up movies. Like many Americans, I'd had a passing exposure to hearing the Mother Tongue as spoken by the Beatles or movie stars such as Julie Andrews and Richard Burton. I'd never had an opportunity, however, to really converse with British blokes. Fortunately, our differing accents caused no major miscommunications.

The staff shared moments of relaxed conviviality. The Reuters office was located on the sixth floor of the National Press Building; the bar in the National Press Club was just above us on the thirteenth floor, so we were only a brief elevator ride away from cocktails at noon and later in the day. My new working mates were lively conversationalists over glasses of Guinness, one of the potions that I never cared for. Guinness tasted unacceptably bitter even when smoothed with a splash of Rose's Lime. I alternated between Beefeater martinis, scotch and soda, and, for a real change, cherry-sweetened Manhattans. The challenge was to determine the drink exactly suited to my mood at the time. I rarely failed to find a suitable one. Any achieved the effect I needed.

My first reporting assignments outside the office were what I considered routine. I picked up press releases and attended press briefings at alphabet agencies such as the SEC, CAB, FTC, and so on. The Securities and Exchange Commission regulated the offering and sale of stocks. The Civil Aeronautics Board, which would become history within a few years, decided which airline operators could fly where and how often and what fares they could charge. The Federal Trade Commission set rules to protect consumers against, for example, false advertising. I never set foot in the one place a person might expect to be covered by a reporter who had spent his younger years on farms in Texas. Reuters had a man assigned full-time to the US Department of Agriculture beat because of its broad economic implications for the nation's farmers and ranchers as well as for housewives shopping at the grocery store.

While the news emanating from such regulatory agencies seldom made front-page headlines, they were bread-and-butter stuff for the economics-minded Brits. Business news was money-generating news. Reuters was competing with Dow Jones to sell its economic information service to banks, brokers, investment houses, and other financial interests. Wherever a Reuters man might be working around town, whether in the White House, at the Justice Department, or even in the Pentagon, he was indoctrinated not to ignore a news item that might have economic repercussions for someone or some company or organization somewhere.

At the SEC I sometimes encountered *Wall Street Journal* reporters who were out gathering news for the Dow Jones ticker. It so happened that one of them had been reared in a Texas town ninety-five miles east of Lubbock about the size of my hometown of Meadow. Karen Elliott had graduated from high school at Matador, something I learned as we shared a taxi back to the National Press Building. My mother had relatives from Matador, including my great-grandfather, the old white-mustachioed Kid Kennedy. Small world, Karen.

Karen Elliott went from feeding SEC news to the Dow Jones ticker to covering diplomatic affairs at the State Department for the *Journal*—and winning a Pulitzer Prize for reporting on the Middle East in 1984.

During almost a decade with Reuters I covered practically every kind and grade of news in Washington and on foreign trips with officials while I was assigned to the State Department or the Pentagon. Three early years were spent covering Congress. I made several trips with the White House press corps trailing the president—first Jimmy Carter then Ronald Reagan—around the country. I had cocktails with Mr. Carter as guest at a private mountain lodge in the Grand Tetons of Wyoming. I attended church in Beverly Hills with Mr. and Mrs. Reagan as a member of the White House press pool.

President Jimmy Carter with White House press members during vacation at Jackson Hole, Wyoming, in 1978 (White House photo).

I covered some of the developments preceding Richard Nixon's resignation, including the trial of the "Watergate plumbers." Those were five characters who were involved in the botched burglary of the Democratic National Committee offices in the Watergate apartment complex. And there were two uneasy weeks spent covering the Supreme Court when our regular court man, Tom Stewart, was on leave. Thank heavens the high court issued no major decisions while I was on the scene. I knew little about the Supreme Court. Latin phrases used in court rulings—amicus curiae, ex parte, and such—would have sent me scrambling to find a legal expert for help. I might have pleaded *ignorantia juris non excusat*, but ignorance of the law would have been no good excuse. I was truly a lost ball in high weeds.

Covering Capitol Hill was generally simpler than covering the other regular news beats around Washington. With a hundred senators and 435 representatives, each having press aides to toot their horns, news or what passed for it practically chased down the reporter, rather than vice versa. Situations abounded that could generate headlines: hearings during which ranking officials might be testifying about an ongoing crisis or societal dilemma, meetings of congressional committees deliberating legislation having effects throughout the nation, impromptu interviews in hallways where reporters caught important figures coming or going from hearings or legislative sessions, and the ubiquitous photo ops. The reporter for a major newspaper such as the *Washington Post* has the freedom to select a single story to pursue through the day or perhaps for many days. Wire service reporters do not have that luxury. We served diverse clients. We scurried like rabbits from one place to another.

At the start of the day, schedules were posted in the Senate press gallery listing Senate committee hearings and House committee hearings. My Reuters cohort Mike Posner assigned responsibility for each of us to attend as many as three or four hearings, at least to get copies of prepared testimony, from which we'd later write stories. Ideally we'd stay in a hearing for the question-and-answer session, but time did not always permit it. I would linger longest at the one hearing that seemed most important—for example, a Senate Foreign Affairs Committee session about the Vietnam War. In three years on the Hill I spent thousands of hours sitting in such committee rooms, jotting notes, patiently waiting for something outrageous to be said that might make front pages throughout the country.

On certain mornings a couple of us correspondents would take an elevator down to the Senate floor to ask Senate Majority Leader Mike Mansfield about the outlook for progress, or lack of it, on pending legislation or the resolution of other congressional issues. We'd be alone with him before any other senators arrived. Mansfield was soft-spoken, courteous, helpful—quite the gentlemanly figure as remembered by millions of Americans who heard him deliver a moving eulogy when President John F. Kennedy's body lay in state in the Capitol rotunda after his assassination November 22, 1963.

In the eulogy Mansfield described what Jacqueline Kennedy had done moments after her husband was pronounced dead. She wanted to leave something personal in the casket in remembrance of their life together; having nothing else, she removed her wedding ring and placed it with the president. In eloquent prose echoed in the marbled rotunda, Mansfield spoke of how "in a moment it was no more, and so she placed a ring from her finger, and placed it in his hands." The thought was repeated four times until the fifth line became ". . . and she took a ring from her finger and placed it in his hands, and kissed him."

On January 15, 1975, Mike Posner and I stood in the press gallery overlooking the House of Representatives as Gerald Ford delivered his first State of the Union message as president. Ford had been Richard Nixon's vice president; he assumed the office when Nixon resigned on August 9, 1974, because of the Watergate scandal. Listening to Ford's address, I found myself thinking of how I'd tracked him down in 1964 at Love Field in Dallas in an assignment related to the Kennedy assassination. Ford, a House member from Michigan, was serving on the Warren Commission investigating circumstances surrounding the president's death. He and other commission members came to Dallas to reconstruct what had happened on that fateful moment in 1963 when Kennedy was shot as his motorcade drove past the Texas School Book Repository.

I somehow managed to locate the congressman at Dallas's Love Field. He was awaiting what I surmised would be a charter flight back to Washington. I spotted him standing alone, clutching a valise, in a waiting area apart from the main terminal. The opportunity was there for me to get exclusive news of the day.

I introduced myself as a reporter with the Associated Press.

"Can you tell me what you learned today, Mr. Congressman?"

"No comment." He regarded me as if skeptical that I was who I said I was.

I started to ask when he thought the commission might complete its report, but another no comment cut me short. This time he stared straight ahead, refusing to even look at me.

I went away disturbed. It is difficult to write much of a story when all you have to base it on is no comment. The congressman had not been cooperative the way I thought he should have been. I didn't think the congressman was being very nice, treating me that way.

The Warren Commission report was released in September 1964, with its conclusion that Lee Harvey Oswald had acted alone in killing President Kennedy. Kennedy's successor, Lyndon Johnson, had wanted such a report in order to ease concerns that others besides Oswald might have been involved in the assassination. The commission's findings at first satisfied most people, but eventually the Warren report, as extensive as it appeared to be, with twenty-six volumes of testimony and analysis, was criticized as a shoddy piece of work. In the last edition of the report Ford said the Central Intelligence Agency had destroyed or kept from investigators critical secrets connected to the assassination. The commission's probe put "certain classified and potentially damaging operations in danger of being exposed." The CIA's reaction, he said, "was to hide or destroy some information, which can easily be misinterpreted as collusion in JFK's assassination."

Although Gerald Ford had irked me with his refusal to answer my questions in 1964, his wife Betty came through ten years later in a different way with comments outside the White House that made a nice story. The Fords were moving into the presidential mansion after Richard Nixon's resignation. The press was told that Mrs. Ford would discuss her ideas about redecorating the living areas of the White House.

When Mrs. Ford appeared on the South Lawn to meet us, I found myself the only male reporter among a half-dozen women asking the new first lady about the move-in. This was not my idea of where I should be to get a barn-burner of a story. Afterwards I did put together a feature-ish little piece. I expected that at best it might wind up appearing in what was then called the society pages. My story began, as I recall, with something like, "First Lady Betty Ford took a look around her new home today and said later she believed she'd take it." Next day I was pleasantly surprised to see my Betty Ford story on the front page of the *New York Times*. Well, now. What a bright feather in my bonnet, outshining a group of female correspondents that included UPI's Helen Thomas on a story I thought sure could only be the province of the female set.

Only later did I recall something I noticed about the first lady's demeanor that seemed a bit odd. As she had talked us, her words were slightly slurred. She spoke in a cautious, almost mechanical manner as if being careful not to make a mistake in what she was saying. I thought possibly she'd had a couple of glasses of wine to ease her tension before coming out to face the questioning. No big deal. As soon as I finished writing I'd be going to the press club bar for something to ease my tensions. I might even stay there for hours, drinking, playing cards in the game room, losing money, drinking some more.

In 1978 Mrs. Ford admitted that she had been addicted to prescription pills and alcohol. It took me years even to hint privately to select people that maybe I drank a wee bit too much on occasion. I kept refusing to believe that alcohol was a problem for Bob Horton. Boozing had not yet led to any major consequences—unless one considered the possible loss of a lovely, devoted wife and the breakup of a family a major consequence. Which, of course, it was.

I staved off that consequence for a time by bringing Sherry and my two sons and Freddie the freeloading dog up from Lubbock in 1974. Tired of living alone in a suburban Virginia apartment, I bought a three-bedroom, chalet-type home in the Shenandoah Mountains about sixty miles west of Washington. That location required driving more than an hour to reach the capital, but the isolated retreat would be a wonderful place for the family to live. I would of course need to be cautious about my drinking and driving. One could never be careful enough about that.

Braniff International Charters

The United States of America National Press Corps

Cocktails

Peru's Pisco Sour
(a Braniff exclusive)
Gin Martini
Vodka Martini
Manhattan
Whiskey Sour
Margarita
Bloody Mary
Screwdriver
Sherry
Bourbon – Old Forrester
Canadian – Canadian Club
Scotch – J&B
Johnny Walker Black
Rum – Bacardi
Gin – Beefeater
Vodka – Smirnoff

Wines

Macon Blanc
Wedding Veil
Pommard
Bichot

Liqueurs

Remy Martin V.S.O.P.
Grand Marnier
Drambuie
Creme De Menthe
Kahlúa
Amaretto Di Saronno
Benedictine & Brandy
Tawny Port – Croft

Beers

Coors, Budweiser, Lone Star

Soft Drinks and Juices

Idaho Falls, Idaho – Andrews AFB, Washington, D.C.
August 30, 1978

Cocktail service	Hors d'oeuvres
Dinner	Fresh Garden Salad/Chef's Dressing
Entrée	Individual Beef Wellington Garden vegetables
or	English Sole Meuniere Garden vegetables Irish potatoes
	Cheese/crackers
	Fancy fruit tarte
	Chocolates
	Colombian coffee/Cappuccino
	Tea Service
	Your choice of beverages from the bar
	Finger sandwiches Open faced Scandinavia sandwiches Petit Fours
	Tea/Colombian coffee

In-flight dining selections for the White House press entourage following President Jimmy Carter on Wyoming vacation in 1978.

15

Flights on trips with cabinet-level officials were what one might expect on US government jets: super efficient, swift, and safe. Each journey was like having a red carpet unfold before you as you traveled. Hotel reservations already were made; sign in at the front desk and get the key to your room. Place your bag outside your hotel room at an appointed hour, and someone would take it to the plane. Sign for credit card charges along the way and calculate later how much to file on your expense sheet for the home office.

Over the years I accompanied several secretaries of state and secretaries of defense to high-level meetings in Europe, the Middle East, and Mexico. A military transport once took me with other Pentagon reporters to Cuba to witness a practice invasion at Guantanamo Bay. Trips like that were strictly business. By contrast, commercial flights chartered for White House reporters trailing the president's Air Force One on trips out of Washington could be lively, especially on a return leg after the major work was behind us. Booze was available as soon as you set foot inside the plane. A rolling cart at the cabin door was stocked with iced glasses of Bloody Marys and screwdrivers along with the usual rows of bottled wine and miniatures of bourbon, scotch whisky, and martinis. It was difficult for me to pass the cart without getting a pick-me-up, even on a morning departure. The bill for flight, food, and refreshments was divvied up later and sent to our offices.

I was careful not to overdo the drinking on those trips. A clear head was needed to write a coherent story to be filed at the next landing. Sometimes so little was going on that producing a mildly interesting piece was a stretch for a sober mind. One needed to be alert in case Air Force One carrying the president should disappear from radars or in case a terrorist or crackpot should take a shot at him at the next landing. Those were dread possibilities.

On March 30, 1981, I had been close to the moment and the scene of one of those dread possibilities. At 2:27 p.m. that day President Ronald Reagan was shot by John Hinckley, Jr., outside the Washington Hilton as the president left a speaking engagement. It happened at a side entrance across the street from a foreign embassy's office where I had just been to submit paperwork for a trip abroad with Secretary of State Alexander Haig.

I'd chosen the morning to take care of the task so I'd be back at the State Department for the regular noon news briefing. Shortly after emerging from the briefing, television was carrying breaking news about the president's being shot. Had I chosen to wait until after the briefing to go on that paperwork errand near the Hilton, I might have been only steps away from witnessing that once-in-a-lifetime news event.

Alexander Haig, a retired Army general, was the second of three secretaries of state serving in the 1980s, when I covered the State Department for Reuters and later for *U.S. News & World Report*. The first was former senator Edmund Muskie; the third was George P. Schultz, who had previously been secretary of labor and secretary of the treasury. Haig tended to generate the most headlines because he was often extravagantly verbose and outspoken, no matter whose cage his words might rattle.

Haig definitely rattled certain cages and drew public criticism for remarks he made as Reagan lay critically wounded at George Washington University Hospital. With Vice President George Bush away on a trip—he had been flying to Texas before being alerted to return to Washington—Haig told reporters in the press room at the White House: "I am in control here."

Haig was not trying to be an ominous "man on horseback" out to seize power in the president's absence, as some perceived his comment to mean. It was a clumsy Haigspeak way of assuring that someone was on hand in that moment of crisis capable of making important decisions. When a reporter had asked who was minding the store with the president disabled, Haig stepped forward to say: "Constitutionally gentlemen, you have the president, the vice president, and the secretary of state, in that order, and should the president decide he wants to transfer the helm to the vice president, he will do so. As for now, I'm in control here, in the White House, pending the return of the vice president and in close touch with him. If something came up, I would check with him, of course."

Haig seemed to have a certain sensitivity about his standing in the government. Consequently, he kept a close eye on what was reported about him and his State Department and often reacted. On one occasion that remains vivid in my memory, we were sitting in a plane waiting to leave on a trip abroad when Haig strode toward us from his private area up front and stood jabbing a finger down at the CBS correspondent. "Bob Simon," he said sternly, "you got me wrong!" I was seated immediately in front of Simon and quite in the line of fire. I could tell that Haig was not faking anger. I didn't know what Simon had reported that had drawn Haig's ire, whether it involved an error in reporting or something else that had rubbed the secretary of state wrong. Whatever, I was glad not to be the one strapped into Simon's seat. I had no dog in that fight.

Once, however, I was called on the carpet myself by Haig's spokesman, Dean Fischer, who had been a reporter for *Time* before joining the State Department. His was gentle criticism compared to Haig's reproach of the CBS correspondent. I'd written a story Haig didn't like; Fischer asked why I hadn't sought State's input before writing it. I'd felt sure the department would at best have a "no comment," or possibly try to dissuade me from writing the piece. In any event, I was confident about the official source of my story and made no apology for it. The issue was not pursued further. I understood Fischer's position. A subordinate often is obliged to go through the motions of chiding a reporter to pacify the boss. We all know the game.

Bernard Kalb was on both sides of the game, for years as a network TV journalist for CBS and later NBC, then for a time as the State Department spokesman at our noon briefings. Both he and his brother Marvin were veteran, respected journalists on the Washington scene. Bernie, the more extroverted of the two, had a soundproof broadcast booth the size of a small closet only a step or two away from my Reuters cubicle in the State Department press room. We had ample opportunity to kid around, swap stories, and generally put a little zest into the slow, wait-and-watch times between news activities. His favorite greeting upon seeing me: "Horton, you fascist! What are you up to today?" I'd laugh. I was too soft to be a fascist.

I doubt that Bernie ever felt comfortable in switching from his role as journalist to being the State Department's mouthpiece. Virtually all his responses to questions from correspondents who were once his companions in the press room were rehearsed. The department spokesman had a special ring binder of carefully prepared statements that he could refer to in answering questions at the briefings; it could be risky to deviate from the special lingo used in diplomatic circles. The wrong use of a word or phrase might set off tremors in other world capitals or fail to communicate properly the American stance on an important issue. For example, for the State Department to say that the United States "deplored" the action of another government would be a mild rebuke; to "condemn" the action would be harsh criticism.

The department spokesman might thumb through the pages of his briefing book and fail to respond to a question by uttering a line heard all too often: "I have nothing on that." No amount of questioning was likely to force the man at the podium to deviate from his "I have nothing on that." Higher-ups had provided him with no words to address the issue at hand; therefore, he might as well hold up a sign: *Put your pens down, gentlemen. I have nothing to say about that.*

Some things that State would not discuss publicly might be addressed in private elsewhere in the building if a reporter had gained the trust of the appropriate officials. In 1981 I was curious to know the extent to which the State Department was concerned about Libya's support of international terrorism. Ronald Reagan was calling Libyan dictator Muammar Gaddafi the "mad dog" of the Middle East. I sought an interview about Libya on background with the State Department's Libya desk officer, a career Foreign Service woman whom I judged to be in her thirties. "On background" meant that I would not identify her by name in any story that I wrote.

The lady and I had talked only moments when she let go a nugget of information that startled me. A group of Libyan military officers had been detected trying to get into the United States through Canada; US intelligence had word that Gaddafi had assigned them to go after President Reagan. So far as I knew, it had not previously been reported that Washington knew that Gaddafi was scheming to assassinate the president of the United States.

Rodney Dangerfield could have said it for me: Wire service reporters don't get no respect. Had someone like the *Times* or the *Post* broken news of Libya's assassination plot, the story would have set the whole world in a dither overnight, with comments regurgitating from the White House and beyond. But it took a few days after my story appeared on the Reuters wire for other media to react. Other reporters eventually did produce their own pieces about Gaddafi's assigning a hit squad to kill Reagan. Libya was soon portrayed as a threat to world stability. President Reagan later wrote in his memoirs (*An American Life*) that he had been warned about the danger posed by Libya. Security people, the president said, subsequently obtained "what they considered highly credible information that not only I, but [Vice President] George Bush, [Secretary of Defense] Cap Weinberger, and Al Haig were targeted by Libyan hit squads that had been smuggled into this country."

Five years later, as Gaddafi's regime continued to organize and train terrorists, Reagan ordered US planes to bomb targets in Libya. More than one hundred persons were killed. Gaddafi survived that attack, but his days were numbered.

The years roll on. In 1986 I was a forty-something who had been working in the nation's capital more than twenty years, and yet I still liked to think of myself as something of a young fellow on the news scene. One fine, sunny day I got an indication that not everyone shared my perception of myself. As a taxi dropped me off at the State Department, I noticed several of the fellows standing nearby with pens, pads, and hand-held recorders at the ready. It was a typical stakeout to intercept some big-wig expected to emerge from a hush-hush chat with an important US official. Don Oberdorfer, a top-notch military and diplomatic affairs reporter for the *Washington Post*, waved me over, told me what was up, then introduced me to a new man on the beat for *Newsweek*. We shook hands, and I was flattered that the new man said he had seen my byline, until he also added: "I know you—you're one of the old-timers."

One of the old-timers? Walter Cronkite was an old-timer. So was Ronald Reagan. Elvis had been dead nearly ten years, but I was still above ground walking, breaking big news stories when I wasn't livening up press club card games and other carefree affairs. *Old-timer?* Give me a break! I took it on the chin and went on inside.

The State Department press room was empty but for a young woman who had recently started attending briefings but rarely asked questions. She was a tall, attractive blonde who kept to herself in the CBS sound booth immediately across the aisle from the Reuters work spot. Our chest-high partition in no way hampered chatting with passersby, yet I never once thought to introduce myself to the young lady or even ask her name. I was one of the veterans, an old-timer; new correspondents came and went. You never knew when a new face would not show again. Sure enough, our attractive new neighbor soon did stop coming, but later she appeared more and more on the television screen. Her name, I learned: Diane Sawyer. *Ahem*. I should have begged her pardon for the slight. *We hardly knew you back when, did we, Miss Sawyer?*

16

I was drunk at the wheel, coming out of a mountain grade at maybe eighty miles an hour and careening into the little town of Round Hill, Virginia, when the night turned violent and chaotic. I remember feeling the car sliding onto the graveled shoulder of the highway and hearing the rapid rat-a-tat-tat sound of the right front fender moving down a white picket fence bordering someone's front yard. Then, in a shattering, mind-numbing moment, the car was rolling and tumbling, and just before I lapsed into unconsciousness I experienced a feeling that some horrible thing, some other-world force, evil beyond anything I had ever imagined, was clutching at my very soul. If I never before believed that a satanic being exists among us or in us, I was inclined to believe it after that frightening experience.

When I regained consciousness I found myself struggling desperately to breathe again. *If I don't get some air I am going to die*. A bright light shone into the car. I heard a rending of metal and became aware that someone outside was wielding mechanical rippers known as jaws of life to open the crumpled door on the passenger side. I regained my breath just as the door came off. Hands pulled me carefully from among the bits of shattered glass and shards of metal.

In thc ambulance speeding to a hospital I began to feel pain in my left shoulder and suspected that it might be broken; I would be fortunate were that the extent of the injuries. I became aware of a medical person learning over me, checking my pulse, asking this and that. She was nice looking. I told her that she was absolutely the most beautiful nurse I had seen that night, and where did she live and what was her name? Totaling a car and nearly killing myself a few miles back hardly mattered at the moment. "You'll be all right," she said.

I was seated on the edge of a gurney in the emergency room when my wife arrived at the hospital. A Virginia state trooper stood nearby jotting essentials about me in a small notebook. Sherry said something I wished she could have withheld at that particular moment.

"You've been drinking!" The concerned look she'd had upon entering the room turned to something a whole lot less than. The trooper looked up from his note-taking.

"I think my shoulder is broken," I said. Hospital attendants had my left arm in a sling.

"Everett and Katy are at the house," Sherry said coolly. "They got here this afternoon and we've been waiting for you."

I had forgotten that our expatriate Lubbock friends were due in for a visit.

"Why were you coming back so late?" she asked.

I told her I got delayed on a story. That was a lie. I had taken the day off without telling her. Instead, I went into Washington to play poker all afternoon at the press club. As usual I drank as we played. Our waiter, McCoy, was good about frequently replenishing our glasses.

I managed to walk to the car unassisted. It did not occur to me until later that the state trooper had left the emergency room and had not returned. That was a break. He'd had sufficient reason to charge me with a DWI and haul me directly to jail. Perhaps he decided not to do so because he felt I was punished enough, having wrecked a car, cracked a shoulder, faced the scorn of a concerned and angry wife—all that, with a hangover yet to come.

It was a long drive mostly in silence as Sherry drove us back through Round Hill, past what was left of a picket fence along the highway just inside the town, and on up a twisted rocky road to our mountain home. Everett and Katy sat drinking coffee at the kitchen table. They asked few questions; my red eyes, an awkward apology, the shoulder sling, and a shirt unbuttoned down to the navel said enough. Sherry led me to bed. Our friends left the next day, wishing us well.

So it was at times, ugly, with uglier times yet to come. The 1980s were years of personal and geographic upheaval. Changes occurred as a result of job situations, money needs, and old questioning about who I was and where I should be headed. It never occurred to me that drinking might determine where I was headed.

I doubt that the old-timer label that a younger journalist had given me one day was what spurred me to consider doing something different. Life had been driving me hard—or perhaps vice versa. I had spent close to twenty years involved in the hectic wire service routine, first in the 1960s with the Associated Press and from the mid-1970s to the early '80s with Reuters. I envied journalists who didn't have to scurry from one press conference to another, dashing off one story only to begin chasing a half-dozen others before the day was over. Finding a less frantic kind of journalism became increasingly appealing.

•••

It wasn't a dissatisfaction with Reuters per se that led me to consider magazine work. Reuters had been good to me. The agency had people whose work I respected. Wherever I traveled, I found Reuters correspondents who were closely keyed in with heads of governments and other influential figures. In Washington my British cohorts had a better grasp of what went on in Congress than I ever had of the political scene in London. But I simply needed change.

News editor Brian Bain, always a good friend, called after I gave Reuters official notice that I would be leaving. Was there anything that might prompt me to change my mind? he asked. What about being assigned to the White House? I told Brian I'd decided that I needed a new direction, and, no, going to the White House wasn't what I wanted. I saw an opportunity to move across town to *U.S. News & World Report*, and I was taking it.

U.S. News & World Report was one of three weekly news magazines of the day. "Snooze," as *Time* and *Newsweek* people liked to belittle it, gave its readers a basic bread-and-butter diet of national and international news along with business, consumer, and other items. It was not gourmet, not trendy, not celebrity-oriented. Some smirked at its conservative heritage under David Lawrence, who had founded the magazine in 1948 during the era of fears about communism as "the Red Menace." The magazine seemed to favor hiring people with wire service experience. Lawrence was a former AP man. Marvin Stone, who became editor in 1976, cut his teeth on the wires with the old International News Service (whose merger with United Press formed UPI). Several others had worked with AP or UPI; I knew of no Reuters ex on the payroll.

State Department pal Bernie Kalb, in his inimitable way of friendly needling, said I was engaging myself in what he called "Cuisinart journalism." The descriptive was not far off the mark, considering how magazine stories often were a team effort. If a new Middle East crisis was the focus of the week, the magazine's White House man would put together a file for the office reporting on what the president was saying or doing. The State Department correspondent would report on diplomatic strategy. The magazine's Pentagon reporter might submit a lengthy memo on the military's contingency planning. Those contributions would wind up in the hands of a wordsmith back at the magazine, who'd toss all into his mental blender and serve up a story diced with a satisfying variety of details. His contributors were credited. For example, I provided information for a piece that appeared in the September 16, 1985, issue about a meeting between Ronald Reagan and Soviet leader Mikhail Gorbachev ("President Faces Rocky Climb to the Summit"). At the end of the story was a line crediting the four contributors: By Joseph Fromm with James M. Hildreth, Robert A. Kittle, and Bob Horton. Over time there were other stories for which I did both reporting and final writing, and thus had a byline all to myself. I doubt that such credits meant much to anyone except us staffers; most readers probably paid scant attention to whose name appeared at the bottom of our stories.

Switching from the wire service style of reporting to magazine writing wasn't as easy as I had anticipated. A typical AP item would be taut and cryptic and simply end when the facts ran out. The magazine piece needed to be more, well, storylike, with an ending that brought the reader back to the story's beginning point of emphasis. Length was of less concern; the magazine writer had more breathing space to tell his tale.

Foreign editor Roy Hanson once stopped at my desk to return a story I had turned in, an assigned wrap-up of yet another Middle East crisis. He said I should take another stab at writing it by revising the opening paragraphs. He gave me advice that I tried to remember as time went

Secretary of State George Shultz with editors of *U.S. News & World Report* (*USN&WR*, March 12, 1984, photo courtesy Thomas J. O'Halloran).

on: "You're trying too hard. You need to loosen up." I tried to practice what he told me. If words seemed to freeze as I was writing, I found that one way to break the logjam was to take a deep breath, ponder what I wanted to say, and then say it simply and clearly without worrying about style or catchy phrasings. Simply communicate.

For a time the magazine seemed to be grooming me to write a two-page section titled "Worldgram." The section included a variety of snippets of international news, such as the latest coup d'etat in Africa or a collapse of currency in some South American nation. I struggled in that assignment at times. Here again, someone stepped in with advice I could understand. Down the hall from my little office Gerson Yalowitz had been doing "Worldgram" for months. Seeing how I was stumbling, he suggested that I think of what I was writing as graphic little film strips of historic activity. Had I ever seen the *March of Time* newsreel programs of the mid-1930s and '40s? The question stretched my memory, but I did recall seeing as a kid the old show that combined actual film footage and reenactments to illustrate events occurring around the world. Yalowitz said: "Write as if you are reporting what you are seeing in a *March of Time* show."

I took the advice to heart. Accordingly, items that I chose to have in my "Worldgram" section underlined important ideas and resembled something like this:

> Rioting in Birmingham, Britain's worst in four years, will compel Prime Minister Thatcher's Conservative government to sharpen its focus on the nation's high rate of unemployment. What actually caused the explosion of bombings, looting, bloody street fighting in the decaying inner-city of Handsworth on September 9 is still a matter of controversy. . . . Thatcher's Tories call the rampage a celebration of lawlessness and anarchy, pure and simple. A newspaper says it was an orgy of arson and looting by have-nots against haves.

I might have made "Snooze" a career, but after I'd been on the staff two years a change in ownership brought major changes to the magazine, especially at the main office in Washington. I began to wonder how those changes might affect me.

USN&WR was established as an employee-owned company. In 1974 the magazine's employees owned shares valued at sixty-five dollars. The real worth of the publication and property, however, was greatly undervalued in terms of the stock price. In 1984 Canadian real estate magnate Mortimer Zuckerman, owner of *Atlantic Monthly*, paid $2,842 a share to buy the magazine—making some longtime editors and other employees instant millionaires. Dennis Mullin, a thirty-something drinking buddy of mine with ten years in the company, pocketed six hundred thousand dollars. As a relatively short-termer, I qualified for a half-share, or less than fifteen hundred bucks. It beat being shut out with nothing.

Zuckerman began bringing in his own people to move the magazine in new directions. Some old-timers took the money and ran. Others got notices that their services were no longer needed. With reorganization and staff upheaval the obvious trend, I grew uneasy about my vulnerability as a short-timer. Foreign editor Roy Hanson had been the key to my being hired; when he chose to retire, I really began to feel insecure.

I saw what I thought could be a shrewd solution for my dilemma. The magazine had a regional bureau in Houston headed by Sarah Peterson. She'd lost her number two man and needed a replacement. If I were to bid for the job and get it, I could remove myself from the line of fire in Washington. And who better to go to Houston than a native Texan with considerable news experience, including a basic knowledge of how the magazine operated and what its priorities were—or had been pre-Zuckerman.

I needed to thoroughly analyze what I should do. I'd left Washington once before, only to feel compelled later to return to the place where I had spent almost all my working years. If I left again, I'd need to consider it a return home for good, if that is ever possible.

17

Denial is the hundred-proof effective defense used by someone who is told his drinking has become a problem. In my confused way of thinking, alcohol was a solution, not a problem. It was a way to erase concerns about any difficulty that presented itself or ease any discomfort I felt. My biggest problem was refusing to listen to anyone who said that I had a problem.

A book used in twelve-step programs explains why boozers drink on and on despite consequence. Alcoholics Anonymous quotes this from a doctor who spent years treating alcoholism: "Men and women drink essentially because they like the effect produced by alcohol. The sensation is so elusive that, while they admit it is injurious, they cannot after a time differentiate the true from the false. To them the alcoholic life seems the only normal one. They are restless, irritable, and discontented, unless they can again experience the sense of ease and comfort which comes at once by taking a few drinks—drinks which they see others taking with impunity."

With deepening strains in our marriage, Sherry and I attended a twelve-step meeting where I heard the book *Alcoholics Anonymous* quoted chapter and verse as reverently as scriptural readings. Recovering alcoholics refer to it as "the Big Book," as distinct from the Bible, which is "the Big Big Book." I went reluctantly and somewhat skeptically, although once in the meeting I sensed that something good was going on for *those* people. I went to placate a wife by seeking a way to control my drinking. To actually stop drinking completely seemed too radical a solution.

As is the case for alcoholics, the consequences of my drinking episodes had mounted. Some episodes were near-fatal, like the rolling, tumbling car accident that broke my shoulder that night at Round Hill, Virginia. I'd had another close call driving home to the Shenandoah Mountains at dawn one Saturday after a night of drinking and gambling at the National Press Club. I dozed as a dump truck came over a hill at my Volkswagen squareback; we sideswiped when the VW drifted into the truck's lane. The other driver told a Virginia trooper that he had steered the truck off the shoulder of the road trying to avoid a collision, but my car kept coming at him. Glass exploded in my face. I had bleeding cuts here and there but was not badly hurt.

Some drinking episodes were farcical. Once, after we moved from the mountain into West Virginia, I missed the day's last Amtrak home and had to spend the night in Washington. I played poker at the club until after midnight, then went down to the Reuters office on the sixth floor of the press building, where I peeled off my clothes and curled up on the floor. Around six in the morning I awoke with a great thirst and stepped barefoot outside the office to a fountain in the hallway. As the door clicked shut behind me I was gripped by a feeling of terror: I was now locked out, O-U-T, *out*! wearing nothing but my Fruit of the Looms, with many people soon to be arriving for work: newsmen, ad executives, lobbyists, secretaries and . . . *oh dear God!* I felt a horrendous panic not knowing what to do. If I'd had access to a window I might have leaped to whatever fate awaited me, but all windows were on the other side of other locked doors.

Suddenly I remembered that there was a small interior room down the hallway where custodial supplies were stored. Often it was open. I recalled seeing a telephone on the wall just inside the door of the little room. I had no idea whether it worked, or if it did, who I might call for help. Barefoot and naked I hurried down the hall and discovered, *thank you, Jesus!* that the storage room door was not locked. I snatched up the phone and was surprised to hear the thing ringing automatically. It rang a half-dozen times until, as if in answer to my prayers, a man answered.

"I'm locked out of my office on the sixth floor. I'm hoping you have a key to get me in."

A uniformed custodian soon arrived with a ring of keys. Without the slightest sign of noticing my near nudity, he stepped wordlessly to the door and unlocked it. I told him I really appreciated his help. He nodded and walked away in silence as if what he'd just seen happened all the time. Once in my office, I dressed quickly, my hands shaking and trembling. If there had been any liquor around I would have drunk myself drunk again, taking it straight from the bottle.

Some episodes are turning points, not always for the better. The last hope for our marriage may have vanished when I called Sherry around four one Sunday morning from Fairfax, Virginia, just outside Washington. I had a problem. I needed her to come to the Fairfax County Adult Detention Center. I would explain later.

Arrests for DWI's do not require a great amount of explaining, and I omitted certain details to spare my wife the truth, the whole truth, and nothing but the truth. Which was that I had been out drinking, picked up a female unknown to me, and drove us across the Potomac to the lady's apartment in Virginia. Later, as I returned to Washington, perhaps speeding, though I did not think so, red lights began flashing in my rear view mirror. I stopped the car on the Fourteenth Street bridge. A Fairfax policeman told me to step out of the vehicle. He asked a few questions, including what time it was. Around midnight, I guessed. No, he corrected me, two-thirty a.m. I was told to place my hands behind my back. In seconds I was handcuffed. My thought as the cruiser turned and headed us back into Virginia: How could this be happening? Why?

It was a postmidnightmare that worsened as we rode. I knew being charged with a DWI would be bad, but I also had in my wallet a small plastic packet containing a controlled substance. The State of Virginia once sentenced a fellow to life in prison after evidence of a marijuana cigarette was found in his car. Now there I was, seated in a police cruiser, heading for jail with a packet of cocaine in my possession. It took me only a moment to realize that I could be charged with an offense greater than being found with traces of a joint.

No amount of liquor could have calmed my nerves in those moments before the cruiser arrived at the lockup. I tried desperately to think of some way of saving myself. With hands behind my back, hoping that the officer was paying more attention to his driving than to my squirming, I managed to draw the billfold out of my pocket and felt inside trying to get a finger on the packet. I knew there was a break in the linen lining of the wallet; if I were somehow able to stuff the packet deep behind the lining—.

Once inside the detention center, I was called to a front counter where I had to surrender all possessions on my person to be recorded and bagged for storage during my time in custody. Off came my wristwatch and wedding ring. From pockets came change and a cigarette lighter. As I watched an officer reach inside the wallet to withdraw cash to be counted, I felt as if I were standing against a wall, facing a firing squad.

"Nice pictures," the officer said, examining photos of the family. On a sheet he logged my driver's license, credit cards, and other ID. My heart was pounding as he took the paper bills from the wallet and began counting the ones, fives, a couple of tens and twenties, and then—. Miracle of miracles, the man in uniform somehow never noticed the tear in the linen lining, never found cause to further examine the wallet. My do-or-die effort at concealment had worked. I felt as if I had been spared immediate execution.

Before I was locked away, a female officer gave me a breath analyzer test for blood alcohol, asking whether I took any medications, this and that. By now I was feeling enough at ease to be my usual charming self. I told her she was the best-looking police person I'd ever encountered in a county adult detention center. She said I looked nice, too, "considering." I laughed. She smiled. Charm got me no accommodations better than anyone else received. I was placed in a cell with another Saturday night drunk, a fat, sweaty man with big lips that quivered as he snored, which he did loudly, on and on, for the entire six or seven hours we spent as cell mates.

Few words passed between my wife and me when she arrived to rescue me from confinement. If she was curious about what had led to my arrest, she nevertheless asked no questions. She had seen the consequences building. In my mind I tried to pretend that having a DWI charge on my record was no big deal, but I was kidding myself. I had always felt fairly optimistic about life; now I sensed that things were heading in a really wrong direction.

In time Sherry rented an apartment in Arlington, I remained in a condominium apartment that we'd bought in the District of Columbia immediately adjacent to the embassy of Nicaragua. We had moved from West Virginia to the Washington area to be closer to my work. The condo was among lovely buildings along new Hampshire Avenue, but I often wondered about our location. If ever some loony bombed the Nicaraguans, we, too, might go down in rubble.

By then—this was 1982—our youngest son, Doug, was a freshman at the University of Virginia. Older son Bobby had overcome a divorce following a brief marriage and was embarked on a promising future as a surveyor in Leesburg, Virginia. I was proud of them. The boys were doing well even if their dad was encountering quite a few bumps in the road.

Be more careful what you do, I thought when I found myself alone and living the free life of bachelorhood. I could be okay, Sherry could be okay, things might turn out best for both of us. I had some hope that *U.S. News* would soon approve my request to be transferred to the magazine's Houston bureau. Perhaps returning to the home state would rejuvenate me. Perhaps I would even have a new soulmate to accompany me there. Something had been shaping up.

18

I had been in Houston only six months when to my surprise and great dismay I was informed that *U.S. News & World Report* would no longer require my services there—or anywhere, as a matter of fact. The people who had just taken over the magazine apparently knew of no classier way of telling an employee that he was expendable than by using their own variant of Donald Trump's "You're fired!" If they did, there had been no tutoring of the young hireling who arrived in Houston on short notice to give me the word.

The transfer I had requested came in mid-1985, sending me to work with Snooze's Houston bureau manager Sarah Peterson. By now I was involved with a new lady in my life. Mitzi was a schoolteacher. Little did she know that she had climbed on board for one bumpy ride.

Both Sarah Peterson and I were stunned to learn that *USN&WR* planned to close the Houston bureau. Snooze offices were being shut down in Denver and Chicago, too, as well as a couple overseas. Young Hireling from headquarters briefed Sarah first about the details; I would be seeing him the next day over a chummy breakfast.

Sarah thoughtfully gave me a confidential heads-up in advance, saying she would remain on the payroll for six months or a year to deal with housekeeping details of the closure. It was not up to her to divulge what the magazine had in mind for me. I understood. I was not expecting a bonus and promotion.

The next day I made sure to order the menu's most expensive breakfast, eggs benedict, my favorite anyway. I felt justified in sticking Snooze's messenger boy with the heftiest possible tab, considering how

I suspected he'd be sticking it to me. As I clinked my fork here and there in the plate, he outlined the future basically as he explained it to Sarah, but without getting around to saying how I was affected. It was left to me to raise the question: What about Bob?

His exact two words, flat, emotionless: "You're out."

"I'm out," I repeated. It was not as if I did not comprehend the message. I was taking time to absorb the impact. Here I was in Houston with the oil bust of the eighties having thrown thousands out of work, entire shopping centers boarded up, homes in foreclosure all around—and my employer was suddenly throwing me out the door to find a new job. To top it off, this was happening during the first week of December. *Merry Christmas and Happy New Year, Bob*. Looking back, I might have felt better had I given Magazine Messenger Boy a good Texas blessing: To hell with you and the horse you rode in on. I said no such thing. I seldom could verbalize a suitably stinging response at the moment one was clearly warranted.

"They did give me three months severance," I told my new partner Mitzi later. That would give me breathing space to scout out a new place to land. I had no clue where that might be, but Houston in its depressed state was not a good locale. Would Lubbock be a possibility? Should we head back to Washington?

Mitzi was the daughter of a stern father who had her shear sheep and do other unpleasant things involved in raising the smelly creatures on their ranch near Menard in Central Texas. She had a steadier, wiser focus on life than I could muster. "It'll all work out for the best," she said. The dear woman always took that attitude when life threw a person nasty curves.

In retrospect our pairing seemed to have been something of a setup. I was barely acquainted with Mitzi through visits with my sister Linda in Lubbock. They taught at the same school and shared rides. Linda called me one day in Washington and mentioned that Mitzi was newly divorced and having a rough time coping. I seemed to be handling my breakup with Sherry fairly well, she said. Why don't you give Mitzi a call. Maybe you can give her some advice and encouragement? Well, I said. Sure. Okay.

So I called. Mitzi seemed eager to talk. She'd been thinking of escaping to the beach to forget things. I could relate, I said, *yada*, *yada*, *yada*, and by the time the call ended we had scheduled a date in the sun. I flew to Austin, where she lived at the time. We drove to Corpus Christi and hid behind sunglasses while we strolled in the sand and wiggled our toes in the water.

Mitzi went the distance for me, literally. A mutually beneficial relationship that began at the edge of the Gulf of Mexico soon brought her to DC. Had we known I'd be going to Houston, she could have sat tight in Texas. But we were eager for a new beginning, so she came. Then unexpectedly the transfer I had wanted was approved, and back to Texas we went, only to discover halfway into a year's lease of a nice home near the Astrodome that yet another beginning had to be made, this time not by our choice.

Houston therefore turned out not to be the solution for my unease. I hadn't escaped the line of fire from the situation I'd seen developing under the magazine's new ownership. Nor was the work in Houston that satisfying. Much of the reporting done by people in outlying bureaus was contributory; we were often concocting a few lines for use in a story being stitched together in Washington, such as quotes from local folks telling how they were coping with their financial problems. It was good that I'd never had my heart set on winning a Pulitzer or being interviewed on *60 Minutes* for writing some grand exposé. With the magazine it wasn't likely to happen, working as we did in "Cuisinart journalism."

On one occasion I flew here and there around the Lone Star State with Governor Mark White, a Democrat. He was coming up for reelection facing former governor Bill Clements, a Republican whom White had upset in 1982. What I reported from my travels with White was all but ignored in a story put together in Washington that focused on the popularity of Clements. Conservative *USN&WR* wasn't inclined to say anything that might boost the prospects of a Democratic candidate.

Being out of work meant licking umpteen stamps to put on envelopes containing résumés to be mailed to anyone I thought might have use for a journeyman journalist forty-six years along in life. There was no PC to speedily email my qualifications to people. Lacking a thing called a cell phone when I was out and about left me telephonically handicapped whenever a prospective employer might try to contact me; calls had to be made to and from a land-line telephone anchored at the house. How quaint.

After failing to find a job at the *Houston Chronicle*, where Sarah's husband Clyde happened to be the editorial cartoonist, I booked a flight to Washington. Employers generally aren't persuaded to hire people on the basis of résumés or long-distance calls. I knew I had to be on the scene for face-to-face interviews in case opportunity developed.

It pays to have friends, and one was there for me. Dennis Mullin opened his bachelor's apartment to me for three weeks while I hustled about rattling the bushes for a job. Mullin, still a dedicated hand at *USN&WR*, had been instrumental in Snooze's hiring me. He alerted me to an opening on the magazine's foreign news staff; when I applied, he put in a flowery word for me with Marvin Stone, the editor. Stone had high regard for Mullin, knowing how he had performed as a young reporter in Iran, Iraq, and other tough assignments. Mullin was fifteen years my junior, but he and I had been fast friends and drinking buddies. If we weren't emptying bottles at his pad, we were across the street clinking glasses at a stylish restaurant. Le Jardin had become a popular after-hours hangout for many Snooze staffers as they waited to receive scads of cash from Mort Zuckerman's purchase of the magazine.

On Capitol Hill, positions as press aides are often available. I wasn't interested in being the mouthpiece of some congressman who was likely to say or do anything to win reelection. Nor did I consider seeking to return to either of the wire services where I had worked. I'd been there, done that.

I sought out one other former boss for advice. Jim Holland had been Assistant Postmaster General for Public Information at the old US Post Office Department where I worked when it was evolving into the new US Postal Service; he'd become director of communications for the American Association of Retired People. Jim said he was pushing for AARP to subsidize the creation of an AP-like news service to disseminate news on issues affecting the nation's older population; if that happened, he would be looking for an experienced editor to run the service. Jim's idea of launching a Maturity News Service had yet to be approved by AARP elders. Stay in touch, he said.

A more solid lead suddenly came from a former coworker at Reuters who had jumped to the *Washington Times*. Bud Andrews covered military matters for the *Times*. He said the newspaper would soon need a correspondent on foreign affairs. "That's right up your alley, Bob," he said.

The only reservation I had was the fact that the *Washington Times* was a relative newcomer on the scene and was under foreign ownership. The paper had been in existence a mere three years in 1985; it was launched by the Reverend Sun Myung Moon of South Korea, founder of the Unification Church. The *Times* entered the media picture a year after the *Washington Star* folded, leaving only the *Washington Post* to serve readers around DC, Maryland, and Virginia.

Several former *Washington Star* people had taken jobs at the *Washington Times*. That gave me some confidence that it was a legitimate media establishment. One former *Star* man on the staff was Jeremiah O'Leary, a solid, no-nonsense reporter I'd known around the White House press room. Jerry had once been a heavy drinker. Unlike me, he decided he'd be better off giving it up. He had been sober for years. That impressed me.

The editor of the foreign desk at the *Washington Times* interviewed me and almost immediately said the job was mine if I wanted it, contingent on the blessing of *Times* editor Arnaud de Borchgrave. We met with de Borchgrave, who had been an international correspondent for *Newsweek* and later worked for UPI. That went well, but the foreign editor said an in-house problem would keep me from getting on the payroll right away. Because of the budget planning schedule, he couldn't bring me on board for another two months, which meant around March 1, 1986. I made a rapid calculation in my mental calendar. The three months' severance given me by *USN&WR* would carry me exactly until that March 1. *No problem.*

That was the good news I took back to Mitzi, who, with her young son Zachary, was preparing for the Christmas holiday break from her magnet school in Houston. All was well and worth breaking out the eggnog. What had been an uncertain future for us now was packaged as nicely as a gift from old Saint Nick.

Then came a call that threw yet another factor into the equation. It was an offer that demanded consideration. Jim Holland, my former boss at USPS headquarters, was on the phone from AARP in Washington.

His plan to create Maturity News Service appeared to be going forward, and he needed an editor. When I told him that I had a tentative deal with someone else, he was insistent. "Get on a plane and get back because we need to talk," he said. "This is better."

19

In 1986 over thirty million Americans were card-carrying members of the American Association of Retired Persons. The US Administration on Aging estimated that by year 2000 the number of Americans over sixty years old would swell to more than forty-five million, and by 2020 to more than seventy-five million. The growing population of senior citizens meant there was a growing demand as well for news about Social Security, health solutions, money problems, and other age-related issues. Few newspapers were doing much to meet the demand.

AARP's communications director, Jim Holland, had told me in late 1985 to stand by because he had an idea about creating a news service to meet the information needs of the older readers. When I returned to Washington from Houston only a few days after that conversation, it became obvious that his "idea" had been well along in conception and shrewdly conceived: Maturity News Service, as it would be known, would be operated under auspices of AARP but would be at least semi-independent in making editorial decisions about story topics and content. A small staff that I was to head would operate in an office in the National Press Building. The service would be distributed to subscribing newspapers by the *New York Times* News Syndicate, using transmission facilities of United Press International.

Jim explained the plan as we sat in AARP's headquarters on Pennsylvania Avenue. To call it visionary might be a stretch, but I was intrigued by the project's uniqueness and scope. My interest in joining the *Washington Times* began to fade. Going back to covering diplomacy and foreign affairs would mean doing the same old same old. Being involved in AARP's ground-breaking news service would be an entirely new career path. I liked the idea, too, that I would be working for someone whose thinking I understood fairly well from our time together at the Postal Service. I wouldn't have to scope out the style and idiosyncrasies of a new boss.

"Run out and pick up a jacket and tie," Jim said. We were to jump a flight to head to an exclusive club in New York. We would be meeting with key people in the equation: members of AARP's board of directors.

We went, we saw, we conquered. Or should I say Jim conquered, making a succinct presentation about his Maturity News Service at a lunch with members of the board and introducing me as his choice to be the service's managing editor. On our return flight to Washington, Jim described what I should do next. As soon as I got back to Houston I was to make whatever arrangements needed to be made for moving and to let him know when I could be in Washington to begin work. I wasn't to worry about expenses. AARP would pick up the tab. Works for me, I thought.

A merry three-man reunion took place that evening at Dennis Mullin's apartment. Veteran CBS television newsman Ike Pappas had dropped by to visit our *US News* chum. Pappas is remembered in a historic 1963 photograph as the New York radio newsman who was on the scene when John F. Kennedy's assassin, Lee Harvey Oswald, was shot by nightclub owner Jack Ruby at the Dallas City Jail. As Oswald was escorted handcuffed through the basement of the jail, Pappas asked him, "Do you have anything to say in your defense?" At that moment Ruby stepped out of the crowd of reporters and fired one shot with a pistol into Oswald's abdomen.

A few months later, I had been in Dallas helping AP cover Ruby's trial. Pappas went on to report on the Vietnam War, and so did I from the Pentagon. He, Dennis, and I often covered the same military-related news in Washington.

Pappas, having been witness to such historic news as Ruby's killing of Oswald, rarely seemed impressed by anything said or done at the Pentagon. Once as we were leaving a tedious briefing I heard him grumble from the side of his mouth: "Me-go, me-go!" I was puzzled. What did that mean, I had to ask? M-E-G-O was an acronym, he said. It was a way of describing something that purported to be news but practically put a listener to sleep: "My Eyes Glazed Over."

We laughed, remembering such things. Toasts were raised to my good fortune in being able to bounce back so quickly from essentially being fired by *U.S. News*. Dennis suspected that his time might come, but he wasn't particularly worried. He would walk away from Snooze with six hundred thousand bucks, thanks to Zuckerman's buyout of the employee-owned magazine.

More drinks, more memories. Suddenly I became dizzy. The room reeled, my stomach cramped severely, and in seconds I was vomiting, *blah-ah-hhh*, hurling intestinal slime onto the coffee table before us, across my pants, onto the carpet. It was total embarrassment. Dennis grabbed a towel and began mopping at the mess of alcoholic beverage and undigested food all about. Pappas looked on, appearing as stunned as if he had just seen Ruby plug Oswald. I felt my face break into a cold sweat. Dennis hustled me to another room, helped me onto a bed, and had me hold a cloth to my mouth. As he stood back, staring down at me with a look of something between annoyance and concern, he made a remark that I would recall time and again in chaotic years to come: "Bobby Lee, I don't want you to die, man."

I wasn't going to die. I was just sick from stuff I had eaten and drunk.

"You're gonna die if you don't watch yourself," he said.

I needed more than a night's rest. Upon awakening, my survival instincts taking hold, I put away three and only three well-spiced Bloody Marys, followed by only one stiff shot of straight vodka. I was watching myself, just as Dennis suggested. He was off to work and I packed my suitcase for a woozy morning flight to Texas.

"We can't move right now," Mitzi said when we discussed the situation later in Houston. "At least I can't." She felt obligated to finish teaching the second semester of the school term, which meant remaining in Houston for another five months. And it wouldn't be good to pull her son Zachary from elementary school in mid-year. I understood. So began a separation forced by circumstances. In one way that was good, because I could focus on preparing for the launch of Maturity News Service without the immediate distraction of moving a household up from Texas. We were putting together a marketing packet of the kinds of stories MNS would produce for clients. The sampling would be sent to a focus group of select editors in newspapers around the country to get their appraisals of what we'd be offering. I drafted a column on news and issues involving senior citizens called "Lifegram," modeling it after the "Worldgram" section I'd done for *U.S. News & World Report*. The marketing packet also included examples of other items MNS would disseminate: a news piece about the effect of Reagan administration cuts in money for the nation's teaching hospitals, an "Action Line" answering questions raised by readers, a story about cruise ships' beginning to offer more healthy cuisines for seniors, as recommended by the American Heart Association, and so on.

We threw a big bash at the National Press Building to celebrate the birth of a news service reporting on the needs and interests of America's growing elderly population. The guests included members of Congress along with a host of media people. I pretended not to notice the presence of Arnaud de Borchgrave, editor of the *Washington Times*, for whom I originally said I would work. His foreign editor had tracked me down weeks earlier to ask why they hadn't heard from me; I explained how an offer had come up that I simply couldn't refuse, a venture under someone with whom I had previously worked. I apologized profusely, but I knew it was crappy not to have told them promptly of my change of heart.

20

Within a year the *New York Times* Syndicate was distributing Maturity News Service to more than thirty mostly major newspapers. In time the list of MNS clients grew to more than one hundred. In October 1987 Paul Finch of the syndicate's Los Angeles office told us, "I can't think of anything that has sold so well so quickly with our syndicate, with one exception." (He did not say what that one exception was.)

Assigning stories for others and editing their copy left me little time to produce pieces of my own. I wrote one about the old western film stars Gene Autry and Roy Rogers that was displayed prominently in the *Chicago Tribune*. The aging cowboy actors were working together for the first time at a studio outside Knoxville, Tennessee; I was invited by a New York public relations firm to watch them film moments of chit-chat for breaks in their movies on television. I had lunch with Rogers, his wife and occasional costar Dale Evans, and Gene Autry's comical movie sidekick Pat Buttram. I'd once met Autry at the Gene Autry Hotel in Palm Springs, California, where the White House press stayed while covering a Hollywood event for president-elect Ronald Reagan. Autry was a paunchy gentleman who dressed for the Knoxville film sessions in a plain business suit. Roy Rogers, by contrast, was clad in a bright green cowboy suit and sharp-toed boots, appearing for all the world as if he had just hopped off his horse, Trigger, in one of those ancient black-and-white movies.

Another story came straight from down home. My mother and others here and there were playing a popular new card game called Skip-Bo, a kind of double solitaire using sixteen wild cards. The game had

Sen. Claude Pepper, oldest man in Congress at age 88 (1988).

been invented in 1964 by a woman named Minnie Hazel Bowman from Brownfield, Texas, not far from Lubbock. Her nickname was Skip. I called her from Washington—in 1987 she was a spry seventy-one—and she told how she and her husband had concocted the game to fill their hours at a motel where they were staying between visits to a hospital. Seeing how their relatives and friends liked the game, they began traveling around and selling it from the back of the car. The game went on to become a top seller for International Games Inc. and a moneymaker for the Bowmans in their golden years. My mother was proud of her boy for having written that story. She placed a copy of it in one of several scrapbooks she was beginning to fill with other things I had written.

Jim Holland had hired Rob Roy Buckingham, a former editor and manager of the *New York Times* News Service, to be a consultant in the planning of Maturity News Service. I do not know whether MNS was Jim's brainchild from the start or whether Buckingham had come to AARP with the idea. In any event, Buckingham must be credited with establishing a credible structure for MNS by recruiting people with solid journalistic credentials to be involved in its operation. MNS could not be sold to newspapers if editors perceived it as merely an outlet for AARP-subsidized stories. He recruited a group of reputable contributing editors, including Clifton Daniel, former managing editor of the *New York Times*; former UPI correspondent Boyd Lewis, who in World War II was one of fifteen reporters chosen by the military to witness the surrender of Germany in France on May 7, 1945; and former *Times* reporter Edith Evans Asbury.

I suspect that Jim Holland chose me, younger than the contributing editors, for two reasons: one, I had years of experience with AP, Reuters, and *U.S. News & World Report*, and two, he may have thought of me as "his man" in a lineup of mostly Buckingham selections. MNS's regular reporting staff included former UPI newsman Daniel Gilmore and two younger talents, Rick Bowers and Lori Durso.

My buddy Mullin poked fun at Rob Roy Buckingham's name. He said it sounded like the brand of a men's dress shirt. Buckingham would not have found the description amusing. Buckingham took himself seriously. In my possibly prejudiced view, at times he acted like a stuffed shirt. Even in casual conversation he seemed to think of himself as delivering important oratory: chin up, eyes squinting toward some distant Olympian height, lips often pursed between words in contemplation of his next momentous observation.

Pit Buckingham's behavioral aspects against my sarcastic, defiant, overly self-assured traits, and the potential existed for conflict. I felt uncomfortable working with the man. Perhaps it was the difference in years, his sixty-five versus my forty-seven, that led him to have what seemed to be a condescending air toward me. I resented it. I drank over it. Perhaps I was paranoid. But I hear it said that just because you're paranoid doesn't mean someone's not out to get you.

If I had a problem with Buckingham, he had one shaping up with me. With our news office situated in the National Press Building, I promptly renewed my membership there in the National Press Club. Former Reuters coworkers were there. So were card-playing associates back in the club's game room. It was a return to days of old, when I tended to spend my off-hours—sometimes on-hours, too—drinking, bantering, playing poker or gin rummy.

Something must have been said by someone at some time, and I suspected it to be Buckingham. Our mutual boss Jim Holland came upon me in the game room one midafternoon. Work was done. Three of my staff members remained in the MNS office marking time for their weekends to begin. I had a drink in one hand, cards in the other, playing partnership gin rummy with three other members of the press club.

"How's it going?" Jim was smiling as he pulled a chair next to mine. He had come from the club bar with a drink of his own.

"Oh, win a few, lose a few," I said.

"You like to play cards."

"When I win I like it." I felt I needed to make light of it.

I introduced him to the other players. Pleasantries were exchanged, comments made about how good it was to see Bobby Lee back in action. The guys loved mouthing my name. I'd come to Washington as Bob, but once my legal name was known, I was strictly Bobby Lee.

"Bobby Lee is a good man," Jim said. As cards were shuffled for a new hand he patted me on the shoulder and said he needed to be moving along. He was a step away when he paused, turned and casually suggested that I drop by to see him the following day at AARP headquarters.

"Something I want to ask you," he said.

"Problem?"

"Oh, no!" grinning as he rattled the ice in an empty glass: "Nothing really!"

I did not sleep well that night.

In his office the next day, Jim asked how I thought things were going. I said the service was doing well, based on what the syndicate was telling us. More editors were showing an interest in the copy we sent out. Everyone was working hard to make MNS succeed.

"Are you happy with what you're doing?" he asked.

"Absolutely."

"Rob Roy doesn't think you're happy."

I wanted to be careful how I responded.

"I wonder why would he say that?"

"He said you spend a lot of time away from the office."

If Rob Roy thought I was in some way slacking off, Rob Roy was full of crap. I'd worked tirelessly to see that MNS put out a high-quality product. Increasing sales figures showed it.

"It's other people's perceptions we have to worry about," he said.

I didn't get it.

"It isn't just about Bobby Lee or Maturity News Service," Jim said, tapping a pen against his desk. "AARP has its image tied up in this, too."

I did not want to start discussing how and why I felt Buckingham seemed bent on undercutting me. Allowing my irritations with him to escalate into a chronic headache for the boss would be counterproductive. Jim's style, I knew, was to have no appearance of disarray in the ranks. I assured him that I would do whatever was needed to smooth things out with the gentleman in question. I avoided using the term "windbag."

The pen in Jim's hand dropped to the desk. He stood, shook my hand and gazed out the window for a moment before making a final comment.

"Alcohol has ruined a lot of good men, Bobby Lee."

There it was, out in the air. The drinking thing.

"And you are a good man, Bobby Lee."

I told him I appreciated the good thought but not to worry, I knew the importance of handling myself appropriately when I was out and around, and especially at the club.

•••

I found it difficult to sleep yet again. It was obvious that some people were challenging the idea that in my case drinking was a good and important thing. To give it up would mean giving up a part of my very identity. Without drink I was not sure how I would function. They might call it alcoholic, so be it.

Weeks passed without crisis. We'd moved Mitzi up from Houston and soon bought a home in Woodbridge, Virginia, twenty miles south of DC. She found a job teaching in Prince William County. She became the typical soccer mom, and we were out in the lovely rolling countryside a great deal, taking Zachary to practice and compete. Times were good. To keep things on an even keel I began making a few meetings of

Alcoholics Anonymous, with Mitzi occasionally accompanying me. I wasn't abstaining, but I could speak knowledgeably and sincerely in AA discussions about the problems that alcohol created in some people's lives. I intended to see that such problems did not affect mine.

One moonlit night as we walked away from another AA meeting where I had no doubt spoken eloquently about the benefits of sobriety, Mitzi made a comment that perplexed me. Actually it was a bit annoying, although I did not say so.

"Bob, you sounded good," she said quietly, "but . . ." She paused for a moment as if wanting to be sure she expressed herself correctly. ". . . but I think you have this image of yourself in your mind that is not exactly the way you are."

Not exactly the way I am? I believed—wanted to believe, for sure—that I was a good guy with noble motives, sound values, compassion for others and more. But now I heard Mitzi telling me that she saw a distortion in the way I thought about myself. *I was not exactly the way I thought I was?* The comment resurfaced in my mind again and again, yet years would pass before I even began to comprehend the message. Mitzi was too wise for my limited brain power.

21

The 1960 Chevrolet Impala that transported Sherry, three-year-old Bobby Don, and me out of Lubbock in 1961 had been fueled by gasoline that cost twenty-five cents a gallon. Texas Technological College had barely ten thousand students when I graduated with my BA degree. A semester's tuition at Tech had been fifty dollars, which equaled my beginning weekly pay at the *A-J*. There was no Loop 289, and 50th Street stretched near outlying farmland. Bootleggers who once had a lively trade around Lubbock were going out of business. A handful of new stores at an area called the Strip had begun a thriving new business selling liquor and beer.

Just as Lubbock had changed, so had I during my quarter-century absence from the place. I had undergone differing professional and personal life experiences in Tennessee, Virginia, Maryland, and Washington, DC. While I thought that I knew the West Texas cultural environment quite well, I felt uneasy about my reentry from the outer world to the place where I was born and then had so enthusiastically bade farewell. Happiness, as Mac Davis said, had once been Lubbock in my rear view mirror. How would Lubbock perceive this returning deserter? How difficult would it be for me to adapt to Lubbock?

It was a hot summer day in 1989 when Mitzi and I left the northern Virginia suburbs of Washington bound for Texas. She was driving a newer-model Chevy with thirteen-year-old Zachary, a pouty little shih tzu named Ty, and a carload of clothes, some practically hanging out the windows. I grappled with the steering wheel of a U-Haul truck full of household goods. Company for me was a caged canary that didn't utter a peep until we reached Oklahoma and began picking up good country music stations. Then—and this is the truth—the canary would chirp merrily and continuously whenever the sounds of a steel guitar emanated from the radio.

A little bird seemed to be telling me that this time I was returning to Texas for good and that it *was* for my good. I had done the Washington deal from one side of town to the other. All cards had been played. That game was over. I once heard my mother say about me, possibly when she knew I was listening but perhaps not: "Bobby gets bored with new things really fast. He'll get a toy and before long he'll be tired of it and want something else."

Perhaps I became bored after Maturity News Service was launched and the newness of the endeavor faded. Perhaps I overestimated my interest in news of old people. Perhaps I missed the old adrenalin-inducing pace of wire service reporting more than I thought. Or perhaps the National Press Club's bar and game room had been too accessible when I wanted to ease the boredom, whatever the source. Across town at AARP, Jim Holland saw it and ordered a change in assignments. He pulled me out as managing editor of MNS. He said he thought I'd be better off working as an information officer in AARP headquarters.

There was no question in my mind about the change in my role. The switch in assignments represented time in the penalty box for Bobby Lee. The penalty had a look of permanence, given the fact that an out-of-the-way, no-frills office was set up for me at AARP headquarters. Little time passed before I told Mitzi that I had grown tired of Washington. She didn't debate the idea. Mitzi had seen what was happening to me with the drinking and the gambling. Ever a Texas girl anyway, she had no objection to pulling up stakes and making a run for home.

Mitzi and I were now married after living together for many months. It was not a well-planned event when we did the deed in Houston in 1986. A judge had offices in the same downtown building as the *U.S. News and World Report* bureau. He was about to leave for the day when I called to ask about performing the ceremony; I used my magazine connection to persuade him. Mitzi came downtown to meet us. The judge emerged from his office, smiling as he buttoned on his black robe before proceeding to recite the marital vows. His was one of the great gestures in jurisprudence history, as far as I was concerned.

The idea of returning to the *Avalanche-Journal* had first occurred to me when Snooze closed the Houston bureau, cutting me loose in a high unemployment situation. It became a realistic option when *A-J* editor Jay Harris was in Washington for a news seminar and we visited over coffee. I had worked under Jay when he was the paper's night managing editor. He said his longtime right-hand man, Kenneth May, was having health problems and might be retiring.

May died not long after that conversation. The opening had developed, *A-J* publisher Frank Anderson blessed my hiring, and the future was set. My impression is that Burle Pettit's endorsement was needed as well. Burle was in line to succeed Jay as editor in a year or two. He had arrived at the *A-J* as a young sports reporter about the time I joined the paper while a junior at Texas Tech in 1959. He called me in Washington to chat, at one point saying, "I'm kind of sticking my neck out on this." He didn't really explain what he meant by the comment. In any event he must have cast a favorable vote for me. My return to Lubbock was set.

Newspapering had undergone major changes between the time I left Lubbock in August 1961 and the day I returned to work at the *Avalanche-Journal* in July 1989. The old manual upright typewriters that once clattered intermittently throughout the newsroom had been replaced by silent word processors. Reporters no longer pasted multiple pages of a story into a continuous strip so that individual sheets would not get misplaced while being moved to the back shop, where Linotype operators converted stories into lines of lead type. The new offset printing technique eliminated the Linotype operators and their hand-assembled trays of type. Desk editors created images of entire news pages on PC screens; the images were photographed and etched onto thin aluminum plates that were coated with ink as they revolved through monstrous presses secluded deep in the building.

The early 1990s in Lubbock were the most satisfying years I had known since making the jump to Washington in the '60s. Life later would have harsh complications because of my drinking. Nightmarish episodes lay ahead. But in the beginning, the return to West Texas brought me something of a restoration of spirit.

I adapted easily to my new routine of writing editorials and editing syndicated columns. The editorial pages were produced by Joe Hughes, Wanda Evans, and me. Each of us was free to choose the topics and

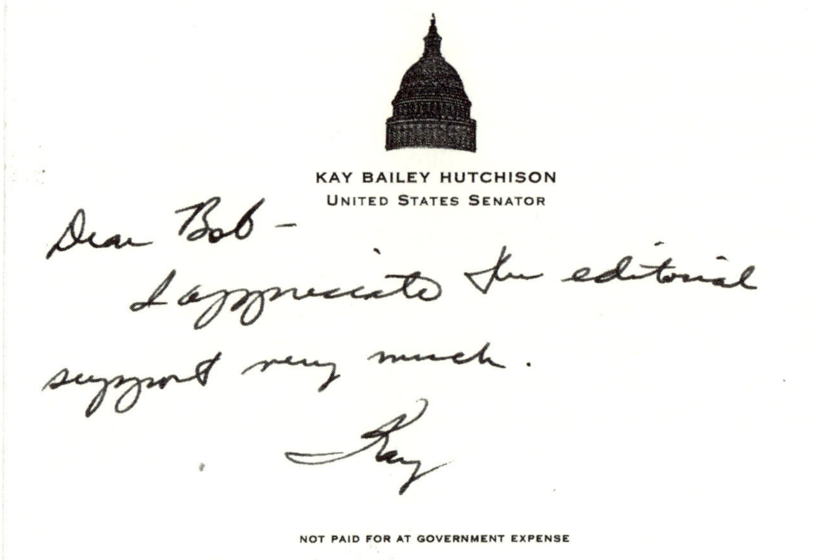

KAY BAILEY HUTCHISON
UNITED STATES SENATOR

Dear Bob –
I appreciate the editorial support very much.
Kay

NOT PAID FOR AT GOVERNMENT EXPENSE

Senator Kay Bailey Hutchison takes note of what she reads in the *Lubbock Avalanche-Journal* (1996).

content of what we wrote, except during election campaigns, when the paper announced its endorsements of various candidates. Not surprisingly, the publisher's views generally dictated key recommendations as to whom voters should be urged to vote for when it came to electing members of Congress, filling the governor's seat, or choosing area representatives to the state legislature. The masthead inside the *A-J* in those days identified the newspaper as "independent," but in heavily conservative Lubbock the Republican candidate almost always won the paper's nod over a Democrat.

Governor Ann Richards, a silver-haired, tart-tongued grandmother who was a Democrat, came to the paper in 1994 to talk to the editorial board about her reelection campaign against young George W. Bush, son of former president George Herbert Walker Bush. Of the elder Bush, Richards once uttered the quote at the 1988 National Democratic Convention that made national news: "Poor George, he can't help it. He was born with a silver foot in his mouth." The lady knew she had little chance of winning the most votes of conservative Lubbock, but she said the possibility of picking up thirty-five hundred or four thousand votes in the large geographic area served by the newspaper was important.

Unknown to Richards, the *Avalanche-Journal*'s publisher at the time, Scott McKibben, had told the editorial board—Joe, Wanda, and myself—that "there's no way" the newspaper would be endorsing Ann Richards for reelection. And so a few days after her visit to Lubbock, the *Avalanche-Journal* urged voters to elect George W. He defeated Richards in the 1994 gubernatorial election and later became president.

I found it particularly interesting that Richards had not been averse to discussing how she once had problems with alcohol. Her disclosing her dependency on booze had not prevented her from defeating a Republican in the 1990 election. By the same token, it probably had nothing to do with her losing four years later to George W. She once said, "Nowadays, hell, you can't hardly get into a primary unless you've done time in rehab."

Besides editorials, I wrote a weekly opinion column that delved into such things as elections, the weather, Texas chili, or whatever I had an urge to carry on about. One column might discuss a current event such as George H. W. Bush's Desert Storm war against Saddam Hussein. Another could be a nostalgic piece describing life when I was a kid, an era so distant that many readers in our college town probably saw it as hoary history. I wrote about my childhood fear in seeing the approach of the dark, roiling dust storms of the fifties. I wrote about my enduring fascination with country singer Lefty Frizzell, justifying it because after all, he was Merle Haggard's music idol, too. I even wrote about a former girlfriend or two.

Becoming involved in chili-cooking contests gave me a refresher course in the grassroots culture of West Texas. How chili came to be cooked by cowpokes with nothing better to eat out on the range, and the antics of us latter-day cooks at our chili contests, provided fodder for a few columns. I went on to write a novel about the kind of fun-loving, hard-drinking characters I often encountered in chili-cooking competitions around the state. *Basic Texas Red* was sort of a comic mystery, which I self-published in a burst of ego and peddled mostly from the back of the car at cookoffs and tailgate parties. Immediate family members bought a few copies. Later I would feel embarrassed in rereading the book. Some parts were done nicely, but the thing cried out for extensive editing and rewriting. I was of a mind to try to recall all copies, take them somewhere out on the plains, and stage a big book-burning event.

If the early '90s were good times for the taking, by the middle of

Senator Hutchison's *Cookbook of Texas Chili Recipes* (1996).

the decade I seemed to be grabbing for too much. The result was a resumption of excessive drinking. As with most alcoholics, I wanted to believe that I could handle a little controlled drinking. For some people that may work for a time, but eventually the old excesses will return. An alcoholic's thinking becomes warped by pride, ego, self-centeredness, and the various other character defects that anyone can have but that are so starkly evident in the behavior of the drunk.

I managed to stay sober for varying lengths of time. Sometimes I might abstain for a few days to try to satisfy myself and others that my drinking was not out of hand. Sometimes I quit long enough to stop be-

WALDENBOOKS

Welcomes

BOB HORTON

Columnist & Editorial Writer
for the
Lubbock Avalanche-Journal
Author of the novel

"BASIC TEXAS RED"

Bob will present his novel AND his own chili for free sampling at Waldenbooks.

Chili Tasting & Book Signing
Saturday, March 2 • 2:00-4:00 p.m.

WALDENBOOKS
South Plains Mall

Promotion of a self-published book (1995).

ing the focus of disapproving looks and comments. I once stayed dry for a year until in AA parlance I "relapsed." It happened when I was leaving Reuters to join *U.S. News & World Report*. I told Sherry that I wanted to take advantage of the between-jobs period to make a sentimental journey to Nashville and visit the grave of my boyhood idol, Lefty Frizzell.

Alcoholics are cautioned to be honest about real motives underlying actions that they will justify to themselves and to others. In the case of that sentimental journey to Nashville, I had more in mind than simply paying homage to an old singer I'd admired as a boy and whose music I continued to play. I was not consciously setting out to drink again, but. . . . As soon as the plane reached cruising altitude and the flight attendant came down the aisle pushing a cart with its little bottles of liquor and more, I made a quick decision. "I'll have two of those," I told her, pointing to miniatures of Chivas Regal. If I were going to drink, I intended to start with the good stuff.

Nothing disastrous happened on that trip. I didn't drink again until I'd been at the magazine for a couple of months. But old promises and old resolutions had been broken with the trip to Nashville. Soon I was again drinking regularly. Cohorts at work drank cocktails or wine at lunch. Feeling that I, too, should be able to drink "normally" put me right there with them.

It had taken Sherry more than a decade to conclude that her best hope for her own happiness was to just let me go. She could see only a continuation of all that had gone on before. I even declared to her at one point, "This is the way I am. I am never going to change." Whether the utterance was an act of defiance, bravado, or outright meanness, I believed at that moment that the alcoholic life *was* what I wanted. I was as honest and forthright as I could be. But alcoholics typically cannot be honest and forthright until consequences start smacking them in the face.

Second wife Mitzi needed less than five years to reach the same conclusion as my first wife: It was time the marriage ended. I did not fight the idea. Mitzi agreed to an uncontested divorce, maybe for two reasons: She was impatient to get it behind, and she was being considerate of me. The only thing she wanted out of the deal was exactly that, *out*. We found one of Lubbock's less expensive lawyers, split the charge, and went to sign the divorce papers.

Divorces surely never go as smoothly as ours went. As we were leaving the lawyer's office, Mitzi said she needed to drop by a fabric store to buy some sewing materials. The store was just down the street. Would I like to come along? It might seem odd that I would choose joining a former spouse to go shopping immediately after a divorce rather than head for the nearest bar, but that is what happened. For thirty minutes or so I stood by quietly while Mitzi browsed among the store's displays of buttons and thread and bolts of bright fabric. Later, on the sidewalk outside the store, we might have shaken hands or even hugged, I don't recall. How we parted did not matter. She had to go one direction. I had to go another.

22

I had paced the streets for nearly an hour outside the Governor's Mansion in Austin, alarmed at still being so drunk at midmorning. I was trying desperately to sober up enough not to make a fool of myself in a meeting about to begin with Governor George Bush. My condition so worried me that I thought of skipping the affair. But how would I explain a no-show? *Avalanche-Journal* editor Burle Pettit had approved my accepting an invitation to join several other editorial writers from across the state for a question-and-answer session with the man. I could imagine no credible excuse for not being there.

The fear I felt that morning came close to matching the terror I had experienced years earlier in the highway crash in Virginia when a grotesque thing that seemed like death itself clutched at my very soul. That moment lasted only seconds before I lost consciousness. The fear of behaving as an incoherent drunk in the presence of the governor and soon-to-be candidate for president had been gnawing at me from the moment I struggled out of bed after a night of drinking.

A truly unfavorable coincidence had started that miserable day. *A-J* publisher David Sharp was ticketed on my flight out of Lubbock for a trip of his own elsewhere. We exchanged greetings in the terminal, but I avoided chit-chat. I made sure to get on the plane after he boarded, hanging back so that he might not notice how badly impaired I was. A passage in AA's Big Book of recovery principles describes what often happens in the life of the alcoholic: He has a "positive genius" for getting drunk at exactly the wrong time, particularly when facing a major decision or heading into an important engagement. So it was with me that day in Austin.

The governor was meeting with Mexico's foreign affairs minister. My fogged condition prevented me from recalling much of what was said. There was a give-and-take about the touchy subject of illegal crossings of the border by Mexicans. Other questions focused on state politics. When it came my turn I threw what turned out to be a wild pitch, asking a non-Texas question about some issue heating up in Congress. Mr. Bush brushed the question aside. He said he wouldn't involve himself in Washington affairs.

After that clunker of a question I could hardly wait to get out, get to a bar, get a drink, get on a plane, and get the hell gone. Just when all business seemed to have been concluded, however, I suddenly found myself in a position of vulnerability again. The governor turned to me, saying: "Let's let our friend from Lubbock have the last question." This was quite a nice gesture, and I suspected that he made it because he had a fondness for West Texas. He was reared in Midland where his father, George Herbert Walker Bush, had moved the family from New England after World War II. The Bushes had personal and business ties in Lubbock.

I blew it. I couldn't think of a good closing question. I bumbled through a clumsily rephrased repetition of the Washington-related question I had asked earlier. Once again, Mr. Bush said he had nothing to comment regarding that. It was an opportunity wasted, when I might have gotten a newsworthy response to a different question. I could have reminded Mr. Bush that West Texas was Bush country and that folks out there were eager to know when he would be announcing a run for the White House. Was there anything he'd like to say about that? The governor probably would have ducked that question, too. He surely would have found a better occasion than a small meeting with a few editorial writers to announce his presidential aspirations. Still, I berated myself for being incapable of asking something besides the off-the-wall Washington question concocted by an addled mind.

Elbert Hubbard, an author of the early 1900s, once wrote, "Life is just one damned thing after another." Poet Edna St. Vincent Millay came along later, saying: "It's not true that life is one damn thing after another; it is one damn thing *over and over*." AA warns the alcoholic against doing the same thing again and again, each time expecting a different result. That is a form of insanity. The alcoholic deludes himself into thinking that he can drink yet again without repeating the consequences of the past. But bad things result again, often to a worse degree.

Call me mildly *un-sane* for trying marriage once again, expecting that the third time I would be different and the result, too, would be different. In 1995 I married Carol, who was half my age, thinking wedlock was the solution to problems that each of us had. She had a baby and needed a husband to be its father. I was in a postdivorce angst, clinging to a year's sobriety, which turned out to be short-circuited with the first flickering of a new romance.

Things went well for a while after a fancy wedding in First United Methodist Church in Lubbock. Then they began not to go so well for reasons any mismatched couple might understand. My large share of the blame for an eventual breakup involved placing the burden on someone else to make me happy. I had been too easily attracted to blonde hair, blue eyes, and, to quote Conway Twitty, "those tight-fittin' jeans." I did come to love Carol's little Wyatt Warren, who I nicknamed WW-Two. When divorce was inevitable, and I drank insanely, my wise AA sponsor, Brian G., said I should let them go and not to worry: "God will take care of that little boy." Ego had me believing that I was the answer to little Wyatt's predicament as a fatherless child. Fortunately, he would in time be reunited with and accepted by his real father in Austin. Brian G. was proved right. God was taking care of that little boy.

The years of the nineties were intermingled with moments of worthiness and waste. I focused on writing to the best of my ability, yet what I produced in the way of columns hardly ever fully satisfied me. Alcoholics tend to be perfectionists, and that can keep them uneasy about what they do. They also can be among an employer's hardest workers; perhaps the last thing an alcoholic will sacrifice by his drinking is the job that earns the paycheck that buys the booze.

My paycheck took severe hits from spending on alcohol. During periods of heavy drinking I consumed a half-gallon of vodka or bourbon every three days. I did not buy the most expensive brands. When I went into a liquor store I looked first at top-shelf items such as the premium Russian Stolichnaya. But, opting for economy over quality, I almost always ended up reaching to the bottom shelf for a plastic jug of some

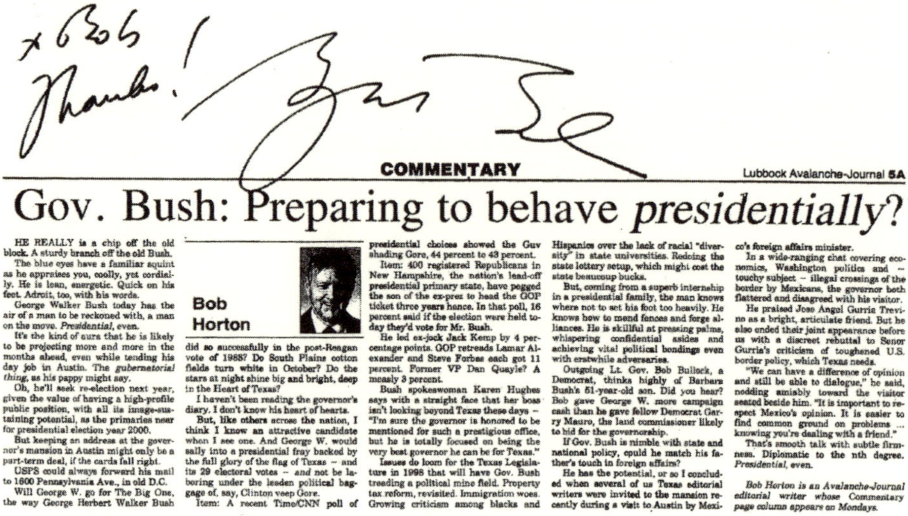

COMMENTARY — Lubbock Avalanche-Journal 5A

Gov. Bush: Preparing to behave *presidentially*?

Bob Horton

HE REALLY is a chip off the old block. A sturdy branch off the old Bush.

The blue eyes have a familiar squint as he appraises you, coolly, yet cordially. He is lean, energetic. Quick on his feet. Adroit, too, with his words.

George Walker Bush today has the air of a man to be reckoned with, a man on the move. *Presidential*, even.

It's the kind of aura that he is likely to be projecting more and more in the months ahead, even while tending his day job in Austin. The *gubernatorial thing*, as his pappy might say.

Oh, he'll seek re-election next year, given the value of having a high-profile public position, with all its image-sustaining potential, as the primaries near for presidential election year 2000.

But keeping an address at the governor's mansion in Austin might only be a part-term deal, if the cards fall right.

USPS could always forward his mail to 1600 Pennsylvania Ave., in old D.C.

Will George W. go for The Big One, the way George Herbert Walker Bush did so successfully in the post-Reagan vote of 1988? Do South Plains cotton fields turn white in October? Do the stars at night shine big and bright, deep in the Heart of Texas?

I haven't been reading the governor's diary. I don't know his heart of hearts.

But, like others across the nation, I think I know an attractive candidate when I see one. And George W. would sally into a presidential fray backed by the full glory of the flag of Texas – and its 29 electoral votes – *and* not be laboring under the leaden political baggage of, say, Clinton veep Gore.

Item: A recent Time/CNN poll of presidential choices showed the Guv shading Gore, 44 percent to 43 percent.

Item: 400 registered Republicans in New Hampshire, the nation's lead-off presidential primary state, have pegged the son of the ex-prez to head the GOP ticket three years hence. In that poll, 16 percent said if the election were held today they'd vote for Mr. Bush.

He led ex-jock Jack Kemp by 4 percentage points. GOP retreads Lamar Alexander and Steve Forbes each got 11 percent. Former VP Dan Quayle? A measly 3 percent.

Bush spokeswoman Karen Hughes says with a straight face that her boss isn't looking beyond Texas these days – "I'm sure the governor is honored to be mentioned for such a prestigious office, but he is totally focused on being the very best governor he can be for Texas."

Issues do loom for the Texas Legislature in 1998 that will have Gov. Bush treading a political mine field. Property tax reform, revisited. Immigration woes. Growing criticism among blacks and Hispanics over the lack of racial "diversity" in state universities. Redoing the state lottery setup, which might cost the state beaucoup bucks.

But, coming from a superb internship in a presidential family, the man knows where not to set his foot too heavily. He knows how to mend fences and forge alliances. He is skillful at pressing palms, whispering confidential asides and achieving vital political bondings even with erstwhile adversaries.

Outgoing Lt. Gov. Bob Bullock, a Democrat, thinks highly of Barbara Bush's 51-year-old son. Did you hear? Bob gave George W. more campaign cash than he gave fellow Democrat Garry Mauro, the land commissioner likely to bid for the governorship.

If Gov. Bush is nimble with state and national policy, could he match his father's touch in foreign affairs?

He has the potential, or so I concluded when several of us Texas editorial writers were invited to the mansion recently during a visit to Austin by Mexico's foreign affairs minister.

In a wide-ranging chat covering economics, Washington politics and – touchy subject – illegal crossings of the border by Mexicans, the governor both flattered and disagreed with his visitor.

He praised Jose Angel Gurria Trevino as a bright, articulate friend. But he also ended their joint appearance before us with a discreet rebuttal to Senor Gurria's criticism of toughened U.S. border policy, which Texas needs.

"We can have a difference of opinion and still be able to dialogue," he said, nodding amiably toward the visitor seated beside him. "It is important to respect Mexico's opinion. It is easier to find common ground on problems ... knowing you're dealing with a friend."

That's smooth talk with subtle firmness. Diplomatic to the nth degree. *Presidential*, even.

Bob Horton is an Avalanche-Journal editorial writer whose Commentary page column appears on Mondays.

Governor George Bush's signature on a column during a visit to the *Avalanche-Journal* (1998).

CominAtCha Vodka imported all the way from New Jersey. The discerning alcoholic knows that as soon as he downs three or four ounces of the stuff, quality is no longer a concern.

George Dub-Yuh, as people who disliked Mr. Bush would call him, came by the *Avalanche-Journal* in 1994 during a hand-shaking tour after his reelection as governor. If he had any unfavorable recollection of my unsteady appearance that day at the Governor's Mansion, he showed no sign of it. When he was leaving, winking and smiling, I showed him a column I had written following the editorial writers' session in Austin. The headline was: "Gov. Bush: Preparing to behave presidentally?" Would he autograph it, I asked? Sure, he said. As he signed the clipping with a flourish I added a very clumsy remark: "After all, you might be president one day." Later I realized the comment might have sounded as if I were saying that being governor did not amount to much. Whatever Mr. Bush thought, he shook my hand and let me off with a grin.

A column on November 30, 1998, brought a television crew to town to film a segment for ABC's news magazine program *20/20*. The column bore the headline: "Here's Johnnie! Crying Racism Against—

Lubbock." I ended up being interviewed for the show. Prompting the network's interest was a false arrest by Lubbock police of three blacks with a women's basketball team from Hampton University in Virginia. The team had come to Lubbock to play Texas Tech's Lady Raiders. The three—two women and the husband of one—were mistakenly identified by a Lubbock woman as perpetrators of a con game against her. The visitors were tailed by police, forced from their vehicle, handcuffed, and held for hours. It was an embarrassing snafu that reflected badly on the city, the police, and the people of Lubbock. When Hampton University retained O. J. Simpson's former lawyer Johnnie Cochran to sue the city, I wrote a column defending Lubbock against the suggestion that the city had a racist climate.

A-J editor Burle Pettit reluctantly allowed *20/20* to come into the newsroom to film my comments about the situation. He did so only after a producer explained why the interview was sought. Local officials weren't talking; with a major lawsuit appearing likely, the City of Lubbock refused to permit any officials to be interviewed about the arrests.

My defense of Lubbock when I appeared on *20/20* prompted letters and calls from minority members saying they could cite instances in which they were affected by racist attitudes in Lubbock. I wrote a second column to air their dissenting views. I also took some ribbing from AA cohorts about my new "celebrity" status. Appearing on television did not quite equate with being "anonymous." My drinking and involvement in AA were not mentioned in the *20/20* program. Thank heavens for small blessings.

My love affair with the bottle was becoming known around the office. When I was arrested for driving while intoxicated in Lubbock in 1994—the second such charge against me since the DWI in Virginia a decade earlier—I felt obliged to alert Burle. I did not want him to learn of it from the *A-J* police reporter who routinely checked the jail's arrest records. As any drunk driver will insist is the case, the officer who arrested me really shouldn't have. After all, I'd only had a couple, I said. Actually it was a couple *dozen* that I had consumed that afternoon at the apartment and that evening at a small neighborhood club. Banjos was a fairly upscale bar with a dance floor the size of a postage stamp. The club's clientele was a fairly reputable crowd consisting mostly of college people, secretaries, wannabe cowboys, wives taking advantage of ladies' night out, guys taking advantage of those ladies taking the night out, and so forth. I believed that I danced like a Fred Astaire when I got tight enough to get loose.

Only because I left the place driving erratically, reeking of alcohol, looking bleary-eyed from booze and a lack of rest, and failing to have my driver's license with me—only for those reasons could a police officer possibly justify handcuffing me for a ride to the clink. Which he could and did. There seemed to be something wrong with that picture.

What was wrong was the picture's reflection of an out-of-control lifestyle that was worsening with time. Did I really think I was concealing it when alcohol in my system affected my behavior? Almost always. The alcoholic is fully capable of believing he is the invisible man. He has a secret. No one knows. *Let's keep it that way.*

For years I had managed to escape legal consequences for driving on highways after drinking too much. Invisible I was, in my mind. That was before Mothers Against Drunk Drivers began pressuring police and prosecutors to crack down on people who took their vehicles out on the road after consuming too much alcohol. A web of consequences eventually ensnares the drunk driver, as it did me. DWI number three came in the hot summer of 1997. I left Amarillo after attending a chili cookoff and treating myself to an unknown but major number of margaritas. On Interstate 27 about twenty miles from Lubbock the red light of a state highway patrol car flashed behind me. I deluded myself into thinking I could magically disappear by pulling onto a side road. I must have blacked out. The next thing I knew I was stopped on a dirt road blocked by the cars of three or four county sheriff's deputies. The state trooper arrived, checked my car for liquor bottles, and drove me to Lubbock despite being informed that he should know just who he was dealing with. And who are you? he asked. I told him. He kept driving straight to the Lubbock County jail.

An overnight stay in the sheriff's drunk tank was not enough of a lesson to keep me away from liquor stores. The next year, after being sent home from work one day when I was noticeably impaired and *not* the invisible man, I went to treatment. Actually, I was taken there, and under false pretenses. I didn't know it, but my AA sponsor, Brian G., had been consulting with Burle Pettit about my problem. I suspect that Burle had a notion to fire me, but treatment was the alternative. So on a

Saturday morning after I had missed a couple of days trying to recover from a spell, Brian came to my apartment with good news: He knew I'd had a rough time and probably could benefit by taking the weekend off for a little rest and recreation. He knew a place to go. Pack up an extra pair of pants, some underwear, a toothbrush and so forth, and socks, he said. He and his wife, Mary, would drive me in their van.

I dozed on a mattress in the back of Brian's van, unaware that I would be away from Lubbock longer than a weekend. After a five-hour drive to the Hill Country of Texas, we pulled into what I learned was neither hotel nor vacation spa but a medical complex near Kerrville known as Starlite Village Hospital. I wound up spending twenty-nine days there with other alcoholics and addicts.

I benefited from my hospital stay and knew I should be grateful for the opportunity to receive it. The respite from alcohol and other chemicals helped me begin to see how I had damaged myself and hurt others in the process. When the time came to leave Starlite, I felt a twinge of sadness in saying goodbye to patients who had become confidants during our many counseling sessions and off-hours together. Something like a homesickness welled in me on the way home.

Starlite's posttreatment assessment of my physical and mental condition surprised me when I finally got around to reading it. I had forgotten some of the ugly stuff I'd done. It probably was a convenient forgetfulness that kept me from ever being fully open about my problems in AA meetings. I still refused to acknowledge the extent of my addictions.

Starlite had this to say about me that spring in 1998: "The 59-year-old white male journalist . . . was admitted to Starlite Village Hospital for treatment of alcohol withdrawal and dependence and substance abuse with cocaine . . . after an episode of acute intoxication. . . . He admitted to the occasional use of marijuana, cocaine and methamphetamines but denied the use of opiates, hallucinogens or IV dugs of abuse. He had three DWI's in the past three years prior to admission. The major psychosocial stressor was that the patient had been unable to see his ex-wife's son." The assessment continued on a positive note: "By the time of discharge Mr. Horton demonstrated a great deal of serenity and embraced the 12-step recovery program of AA and was completely committed to absolute abstinence." That commitment to abstinence was valid through 1998. But by the spring of 1999 a fresh round of ferocious drinking brought my life to a new crossroads. I literally fell from grace at the *Avalanche-Journal* one day when, realizing that I was seriously drunk at my desk and it wasn't even noon, I knew I had to escape. *Get out of here, get home, go to bed!*

Hoping to avoid notice, I walked at a carefully balanced gait across the newsroom, heading for a downstairs exit out the back of the building. All went well until I took the first steps onto the shadowy stairway down. Suddenly I lost my balance, slipped, and tumbled to the bottom against a steel door to the outside. I was struggling to get up when the door opened and I found myself exposed for any and all to see in the bright hot glare of the midday sun. Hands helped me to my feet. People with concerned, puzzled expressions were gathering around. "Maybe he had a heart attack," I heard someone say.

Within minutes I was surrounded near my car by at least a dozen people, including *A-J* publisher David Sharp. He quickly sized up my condition. He wasn't about to let me try to drive away. Take him to the hospital, he said. Managing Editor Randy Sanders took me there. He remained close by for a while at the hospital, listening to my drunken apologizing until a nurse entered the room to take charge. Randy left the hospital, and as soon as the nurse wasn't looking, I slipped away, called a taxi, and got myself back to my apartment.

That awful affair had to be it, I thought. I had disgraced myself for the last time. People at the *A-J* were unlikely to tolerate any more of my alcoholic antics, nor did I expect them to.

I called coworker Joe Hughes and said I was quitting.

Are you sure about what you're doing? he asked.

Yes, I was. I had no idea what I would do next, but I had no intention of returning to the scene of the latest complications I'd created for my life. I was giving up. I probably had given up long before that moment of resignation.

Being jobless and idle was no recipe for recovery. I had unlimited time to think and to drink. I withdrew several thousand dollars from a retirement account. I could get by without working for a while. Despite having resources and trying to convince myself that things were not all that bad, I grew restless. A type A overachiever can tolerate only so much sitting around thinking, even while drinking. I had to be out and about, and that again had its consequences.

During a five-day period in April 1999 I received two more DWIs—my fourth and fifth—in New Mexico and Texas. Those went on file with the long-ago charge in Virginia, my arrest upon leaving Banjos night club in Lubbock in 1994, and the DWI offense filed against me after bing caught drunk at the wheel after leaving the Amarillo chili cookoff in 1997.

Freedom's just another word for nothing left to lose, so Janis Joplin sang. Wrong. Freedom itself will be lost if a driver persists in hitting the highway with a belly full of booze, as I was doing again and again. In Texas, a person who gets a third DWI finds himself in serious conflict with the law. Get any additional DWIs and, as good ol' West Texas boys might put it, you can find yourself in some seriously deep shit.

I was scheduled to appear before a Texas judge in November 1999. I knew I had best prepare myself for being sentenced to time in prison. There was a strong possibility it could be for years.

23

"Bobby, I don't know what makes you drink so much," my mother once said. "Your daddy wasn't an alcoholic." Mama saw something serious developing before it ever occurred to me that my drinking was in any way extreme. Faye and Coonie Horton were never drinkers, as the term might connote for some people. They didn't go to bars to down one cocktail after another. They weren't party-goers who stayed until the booze ran out and the hostess sent everyone home. They didn't make it a point to determine, as I did, whether alcohol would be served at whatever event they attended. Liquor was not a factor in their lives until it became a factor in mine.

Only once in my life did I see alcohol in our home. Two cans of Coors were placed in the refrigerator after my parents returned from a trip to New Mexico. The beers remained untouched for days until a certain member of the family snuck in and drank them. I was a high school sophomore. Those were the days before pop-tops came along. An opener, which we called a church key, was used to puncture a hole in the can to drink from. Salt sprinkled on the top of the can created a head of foam that tickled the nose. Fascinating, this business of drinking. I don't recall Mama or Daddy asking where the two beers went, but they had to know. I think they knew that as a young man I was going to be adventuresome. They chose not to make it a big deal.

It was a big deal as I grew older. In March 1999 I had to be taken to treatment for a second time at Starlite Village Hospital in the Kerrville area. That came after I'd performed my drunken swan dive down the stairs at the *A-J* and resigning to avoid being fired. But no sooner had I returned to Lubbock after twenty-eight days at Starlite than the drinking resumed, this time with catastrophic results.

On a Monday only eight days after my discharge from treatment, a New Mexico state trooper stopped me for improper driving about twenty miles from the little resort town of Ruidoso. I was out to display my genius at cards by playing blackjack at the Inn of the Mountain Gods, or, as I had come to call the casino, the "Inn of the Godless Mountain." The trooper had other plans for me. Seeing my condition as well as an open liter of Fleischman's vodka beside me in the front seat, he snapped handcuffs on me and we headed for the jail. Facing me now was DWI number four, and as if that were not bad enough, I would soon be looking at a fifth drunk driving offense.

After spending the night in the jail at Ruidoso, I arranged bond, paid a hundred-dollar tow charge to get my car back from a garage, and returned to Lubbock feeling as morose and beaten down as I had ever been. It was only a matter of time, a very short time, until I discovered that I was fully capable of making life even worse.

Five days later, Saturday, April 17, 1999, I found myself encountering another state trooper with a narrow-minded view of people who take the wheel of a car while intoxicated. This time I was driving from Lubbock to Dallas to visit a young friend whom I had met during my stay at Starlite in March. Emilie had called that morning to ask, "Are you still coming?" I'd been drinking nonstop since being busted in New Mexico and forgot plans we had made, but *oh yes,* I said nonchalantly. Soon I was heading out on the six-hour drive to Dallas with another liter of liquor to help me along.

Two hours later, beyond Abilene, I must have blacked out from too many pulls on the bottle. Next thing I knew, I was stopped on the side of I-20 outside Weatherford with several Parker County sheriff's cars in front and behind me. They were awaiting a Texas trooper, who came shortly and began writing the citation for DWI number five. As he finished writing, a deputy walked up with a joint of marijuana that was in a cigarette pack that I'd casually tossed onto the dashboard. That added a possession charge to the legal mess mounting against me.

They said I sounded a lot like Johnny Cash when I awoke on a cold concrete floor and started singing with a group of other visitors in the drunk tank of the Parker County jail. I told them I was friends with

Waylon Jennings and could have gone to Nashville if I'd wanted. But, I said, I chose to become a writer instead of a country singer. The part about being a writer didn't impress them as much as the possibility I could have recorded hit songs with Waylon Jennings.

When I was able to call my friend Emilie for help, she said she would bail me out on one condition: I would have to return to Starlite immediately for another round of recovery treatment. Yes, of course, absolutely, *yes, yes*. I would agree to shave my head and dance around airports like a Hare Krishna to get sprung from Parker County's iron hotel. The ambience of where I was was not that wonderful, the fine camaraderie notwithstanding.

Starlite Village Hospital, my temporary sanctuary for the third time in thirteen months, was situated on sixty acres of Texas Hill Country southeast of Kerrville. The place accommodated as many as five dozen patients. I called us inmates. Steps away were a separate dining hall and a picturesque stone chapel for daily meditations and a Sunday service. Starlite had been operated since 1961 by Dr. Francis Eugene Seale, a native of Lamesa, Texas. He had once lost his medical license because of drinking but later became quite well known for helping alcoholics to recover. Under his direction Starlite became the oldest freestanding addiction recovery center in Texas. It was not unusual to come upon cars in the Hill Country with bumper stickers that read, "Honk If You Know Doc Seale."

Our daily routine at Starlite included an hour-long meeting before lunch with Doc Seale. He would read us one of the first-person stories from AA's Big Book and then direct questions around the room asking how each of us was doing, what was going on in our heads, what we felt we should talk about. Sometimes he would tell about his own reckless past to illustrate a point.

Doc Seale once had a practice in West Texas that principally involved excising gall bladders from people, whether such surgery was needed or not. He often drove into Lubbock for a good time and regularly got thrown into jail for being drunk. He said that after one particular episode, the *Lynn County News* headlined a story about his being arrested in type as huge as was used at the end of World War II. Doc said the headline read something like "Local Doctor Goes on a Tear." His escapades were exposed several times in the paper until a day came when his most recent arrest was not reported at all. Soon afterward, Doc said he found himself at a social event attended by the editor of the paper. Feeling obliged to introduce himself, he thought it proper to thank the editor for not publishing yet another story about his being locked up again. The editor replied coolly: "Well, frankly, it's just not news anymore."

Over time, people around Lamesa and nearby Tahoka had become well aware of his behavior. When asked who was the best doctor around, they'd say, "Doc Seale when he's not drunk." Who's next best? "Doc Seale when he is drunk."

Doc Seale had a special feeling for patients from West Texas. He came across me shuffling down a hallway one morning during my first excursion to Starlite in 1998. After introducing himself, he glanced over papers describing my chemical addictions and personal background, then said much too earnestly: "I hear you're a really important man up there in Lubbock."

It was a not so subtle way of puncturing an alcoholic ego. The truth was I had never felt less important, standing there as a prime example of what drinking can do to a person endowed with a supremely egotistical, self-centered personality.

A cornerstone principle of the AA program emphasizes the need for an alcoholic to experience "ego deflation in depth," because "any life run on self-will can hardly be a success." Recovery from almost any addiction hinges on acceptance of a "higher power," a god of one's own understanding to direct his thinking. I was experiencing that deflation of ego, facing court appearances for my fourth and fifth DWIs. I certainly needed some higher power to get my fanny out of the legal fire I had created for myself. A fourth DWI conviction could send me to prison for ten years. I could only imagine how many decades I'd face for a fifth offense.

Oddly enough, becoming acquainted at Starlite with one of the biggest swindlers in Texas history led to a flicker of hope that penalties in my future might not be as severe as I feared. Billie Sol Estes had arrived at the treatment facility pushing a wheelchair transporting an alcoholic friend desperately in need of care. The name Billie Sol was recognizable by almost anyone who kept up with the news in the late 1950s and '60s. He had been convicted of banking and farm frauds of such magnitude that they jeopardized the political careers of important people who had financial or personal ties with him. Those included two Texans in Washington: Senate Majority Leader Lyndon Johnson and Senator Ralph Yarborough. Billie Sol's legacy was such that decades later the *New York Times* would be taking note of his death. The obituary of May 14, 2013, said his rise and fall had been one of the sensations of the postwar era, "the saga of a good-ol'-boy con man who created a $150 million empire of real and illusory farming enterprises that capitalized on his contacts in Washington and the gullibility and greed of farmers, banks and agriculture businesses." Billie Sol went to prison three times. The first time was for a scheme involving phantom anhydrous ammonia fertilizer tanks that he used as collateral to obtain millions of dollars in loans, some of them written in Lubbock.

Coincidence or irony, I had been tempted to work for the great wheeler-dealer in the summer of 1961. I told Billie Sol about it one morning over breakfast at the home of the friend he had brought to Starlite for help. I had been working at the *Lubbock Avalanche-Journal* during my final semester at Texas Tech when City Editor Henry Matthews left to help Billie Sol launch a newspaper in Pecos. The local *Pecos Independent and Enterprise* was printing nasty items about his shenanigans; he wanted his own paper to report his side of the story. Billie Sol assured his associates in the Church of Christ that the things being written about him were not true. Former city editor Matthews offered to double the money I was paid at the *A-J*, which was seventy dollars a week, if I would join him in Pecos, do sports, and help him get Billie Sol's newspaper going. I seriously considered the offer, but I was too close to graduating to drop out of school.

Mike Cochran, who was the AP correspondent at Fort Worth when I was in the Dallas bureau, wrote about Billie Sol over the years, and they, too, became acquaintances. Mike said that in his more than thirty years as a journalist he never met anyone as colorful and offbeat as Billie Sol Estes. As for me, I found Billie Sol to be the most persuasive individual I'd ever spoken with, bar none. He was no slick, shifty-eyed character but a man who could be compellingly persuasive in a quiet, earnest way. Had Billie Sol himself been the one trying to recruit me in 1961, I just might have left Tech to help him establish his mouthpiece of a newspaper in Pecos.

That flicker of hope I got from Estes at Starlite came when he offered to check records of the legal mess facing me. I was hoping my fourth DWI in New Mexico would not be recorded in time to be known in Texas when my fifth case came up later in the year. If that were the case, maybe I could avoid big-time jail time. When Estes returned from checking wherever it was he checked, the news astounded me. Not only had the New Mexico case not been reported, but the records he had accessed showed only one DWI conviction against me at all. That was in Texas. None in Virginia, none in New Mexico—this was despite the fact that I had a first-hand witness who could testify that I had five convictions: *moi,* as they say in Paris.

All that had happened to me—the perpetual drunkenness, the arrests, the walking away from a career I relished—weighed heavily on my mind during that third trip to treatment. It was an emotional thing beyond self-pity, the internal whining that rose up in me again and again. I was experiencing a deep leveling of pridefulness. AA would tell me that very process was necessary to my recovery. Still, it felt awful. I'd been a correspondent for two major wire services, writing stories published around the world, with a byline recognized by my peers and influential figures in Washington. I'd reported for a reputable news magazine. I had been editor in the launching of a syndicated news service. I had much in my mind to assure me I had been there, done that, impressed the crowd, won more than a normal share of the world's applause. Now I hunkered in a dungeon of self-made misery.

The picture-perfect chapel on the grounds at Starlite Village Hospital became a place to ponder the past and try to envision a future. I would go alone at dawn to the little stone structure with the stained glass window that glowed behind the pulpit. I made a habit of getting there before anyone else was around, because once inside the doors I'd begin sobbing like a child. It was a scene I wanted no one to witness: a rubbery-faced, overweight, fifty-nine-year-old man with unruly graying hair, tears streaming down his cheeks, murmuring little moans and fragments of prayers. *Why me, Lord? What now, Lord?*

Not to put too fine a point on it, but I was undergoing the ego deflation in depth as described by AA founder Bill Wilson. Only later would I sense that a psychic change had been triggered in those emotional moments in an empty chapel. It was no sudden burning bush experience. It was the beginnings of a rearrangement of thought patterns and behavioral tendencies that would have beneficial effects for me as time went on.

I still needed a lawyer to defend my interests. A former high school classmate at Meadow came up with a name. Roger Henry was a big ol' redheaded buddy who played tackle on our football team in 1957. He had beaten me by a fraction of a point for salutatorian of our eighteen-member senior class, something I was sure could have happened only through point-shaving in the principal's office. Rog was a certified public accountant at Ranger, Texas, and no stranger to booze or to legal problems of his own; he knew people in nearby Parker County, where I was to appear in court. The lawyer he suggested handled a lot of DWIs. He was also a longtime member of AA. I took the ball and ran with it.

24

An unseasonably warm autumn sun radiated against the steps of the Parker County courthouse where I stood waiting for my lawyer's arrival in November 1999. Anxiety more than heat had me sweating. I had just returned from New Mexico after resolving DWI number four by serving a mandatory three nights in jail, paying a thousand-dollar fine, and agreeing to perform forty hours of community service. Now I was about to appear in court in Weatherford, Texas, for my hearing on the Texas charge of driving while intoxicated. That DWI number five had been hanging over me since April. Billie Sol Estes had said he could find only one other DWI case against me on record, which had occurred in Lubbock. I was hoping against hope that the State of Texas had not yet been informed of my recent conviction in New Mexico.

Even if that were to be the case, what I learned upon arriving in Weatherford threatened to tilt the scales of justice against me to a worse degree than I had imagined. A trial was pending in another case involving a drunk driver who had run into a car and killed four girls who were cheerleaders and basketball players at Brock High School in Parker County. People were irate. The community wanted any and all drunk drivers to be given stiff prison sentences, if not taken out and hanged. I could feel a noose tightening around my neck.

Nolan Queen was the lawyer scouted out by my former high school chum Rog Henry. I liked the man from the moment we met. He had years of legal experience; he also had been active in AA for two decades. Most important, he seemed genuinely interested in helping me, even though I had only a limited part-time income. I had recently moved to an apartment in Dallas and had found work selling subscriptions to the *Dallas Morning News* in stores and events in the Dallas–Fort Worth area. The classified advertisement in the paper said a go-getter could earn a thousand bucks a week. I earned about half that most of the time. I committed myself to paying Queen a hundred dollars a month. He never once said what he expected to be paid, or when.

Queen was shaking his head as he met me at the courthouse steps. He had not been able to talk to the county district attorney about my case. "They've been totally preoccupied with the DWI fatality trial coming up." He thought he might have a chance to learn what consequences I was facing if he could talk to the prosecutor before the judge arrived. I would wait outside.

I lit one Marlboro after another, concluding that I'd done all I could to prepare for the moment. I had called my sons, Bobby in Maryland and Doug in Virginia, to tell them I was likely to get jail time. I wanted to assure them I was mentally and emotionally prepared for that eventuality, and I was. I had resolved to go through whatever was necessary to get my life back in order. I had a wishful thought that I might draw a sentence of as little as six months. That, I would eventually realize, was truly misguided thinking.

My lawyer's expression when he returned gave me no indication whether he was disappointed or pleased, satisfied or shocked by what he had learned from the prosecutor. "Well, good news and bad news," Queen said. The bad news was I'd be fined one thousand dollars and ordered to perform forty hours' community service, the same as New Mexico's sentence. The good news: No jail sentence. *No time behind bars?* That astounded me. I was thanking him profusely when I saw that he wasn't smiling.

"I wasn't able to ask about the possession charge."

The moment of exhilarating relief turned to gloom. Suddenly it occurred to me what probably was going on. I would escape jail time for the DWI, but they were going to slam me hard for the possession of the joint found in the cigarette pack in the car. "Stay here while I check on that." Queen was returning to the courtroom to try to determine how the district attorney's office planned to deal with the pending drug charge.

I set fire to another Marlboro and was not even half-finished smoking it when Queen reappeared. With the same expressionless face, same quiet tone, he said: "They're dropping it."

They were doing *what?*

The county attorney had chosen not to press the possession charge. I was incredulous. It was as if the heavens had opened and showered me with the mother of all miracles. After being so convinced I would soon be going to bed behind bars, I was instead about to walk away from that courthouse a free man.

Queen finally showed a trace of a smile. The prosecutor had given no explanation as to why he'd chosen to handle the case as he did. Maybe, Queen surmised, the people in the district attorney's office were focusing so much on convicting that drunk who killed four high school girls that they were clearing the decks of lesser cases like mine.

I had to go pee, fast. Queen nodded and smiled as I rushed away. I did need the restroom, but I headed first to a telephone to call my sons with the news. They, too, were relieved.

I had avoided telling my mother that her baby boy was appearing in some court and might wind up shackled on a bus bound for the slammer. Mama was seventy-nine years old and developing health problems. She had anguished about my drinking. I decided not to burden her further by revealing how close I had come to being sentenced to a stretch behind bars. She sounded groggy and a bit addled when I called her in Lubbock as if merely to chat. Her pills made her sleepy, she said. I knew she frequently used hydrocodone for headaches. She'd said she had an older lady friend who also relied on them for pain relief. My brother Joe lived in Plano, north of Dallas; I had settled in the Fort Worth suburb of Bedford. We often checked with Mama by telephone to see that she was doing well. Because she had several friends in Lubbock who saw her often, we tended to count on them to inform us about her well-being. Her sounding groggy did not overly concern me, even though I had a fleeting thought that it might be caused by use of the pain pills.

Reprieve was the only word for what had just been given me on that November day in Weatherford, Texas. I had gotten a reprieve when I might have been condemned to years in prison. I had pondered that bleak possibility for months. Before my decisive court date Doug had flown from Virginia to Texas to tell me bluntly, "Daddy, we're going to start making some decisions for you. It's obvious you can't make them yourself."

It was definitely an ego-deflating moment for me as a parent. I always thought I should have the answers to all questions. Here I was being told by my youngest offspring I was incapable of running my own life.

"What is it, Daddy, that you want?" Doug soon asked.

That was a difficult question. After pondering it only for seconds I responded in a way that might have been as profound and as truthful as anything I had ever said. "I don't want to die drunk," I said. And I wanted Doug and his brother to know that nothing is forever, not the good times, not the bad times. We'll get through it all. *This too shall pass*.

If it sounded ridiculously biblical, even if it reflected pure bravado about myself, I felt I was being as gut-wrenchingly honest as I possibly could be.

Doug was on a mission to find long-term treatment for me. He was thinking not of just another twenty-eight-day recovery program, but one extending for one or even two years. We called around the Dallas–Fort Worth area as well as Abilene to the west. We visited one live-in situation in Fort Worth where individuals engaged in intensive recovery sessions and were required to find jobs paying enough money to cover their treatment. With Doug needing to return to his job in Virginia as soon as possible, I assured him that I would enter one of the programs we had investigated as soon as an opening became available. That was a genuine commitment, but I needed to inform my lawyer, Nolan Queen, what my son and I had decided I should do.

Queen was quick with an emphatic no. Entering a treatment center before going to court would be seen as a transparent way of dodging the judicial process, he said. Even if I were to reenter treatment, the DWI and possession charges wouldn't just disappear. They would still be pending against me. I called Doug to explain the points raised by my lawyer. He didn't debate the issue. I added a thought of my own. However long I might be in treatment, once I was discharged the onus to stay sober would still be on me. The responsibility for refusing the temptation of the bottle would ever be mine. I would need continuous involvement in AA to help me fulfill that responsibility.

•••

A thought occurred to me later that soon became a firm resolve. The year 2000 was approaching. I had drunk throughout most of four decades of the current century. I decided that I should and could stop drinking. The Parker County reprieve that spared me major time in jail opened the way to a better way of life. Out with the old, in with the new was the shining ideal. I vowed not to drink again in the new millennium. Y2K could mark a new beginning.

The first printing of Alcoholics Anonymous in 1939 contained a letter to AA cofounder Bill Wilson from a prominent doctor in the field. The doctor said alcoholism was no simple "moral issue" to be resolved by willpower alone. The cunning, baffling nature of alcohol rendered certain people powerless to stop drinking once they started. For the alcoholic to put aside the bottle required the help of a "higher power," which meant a God of his or her understanding.

"Men and women drink essentially because they like the effect produced by alcohol," Dr. William Silkworth wrote. "The sensation is so elusive that, while they admit it is injurious, they cannot after time differentiate the true from the false. To them their alcoholic life seems the only normal one. They are restless, irritable and discontented, unless they can again experience the sense of ease and comfort which comes by taking a few drinks—drinks which they see others taking with impunity."

Being constantly irritable and discontented is not the normal condition. I once heard a fellow AA member explain to a group his simple clue to maintaining sobriety: "When you're feeling abnormal, get off your ass and do something normal!" Doing what normal people do had been the plan when I first moved from Lubbock to the suburbs of Fort Worth in 1999. I had two priorities: keeping the drinking below the disaster level, and finding a job that paid something. The jobs I found were not those sought by a college graduate with years of experience in a profession of some prestige. For a time I packed bottles of over-the-counter pills into small display cases in an assembly-line setup requiring swiftness of the hands and little else. I tried selling cemetery gravesites, all the while wondering, *Am I really doing this?* Later still, I, the former award-winning reporter, had to dig deep for enthusiasm about hawking newspaper subscriptions on sidewalks and in drugstores, supermarkets, and Dollar Generals and once amid the roar of racing cars at the Texas Motor Speedway. If those part-time jobs were not exactly soul-satisfying, they did require me to show some humility.

The pill-packing work at a pharmaceutical company was a team effort that could have easily morphed into a comic reality show. I and a young woman were the token white employees in a group of six, any of whom could have been a grandchild of mine. There were two stolid Vietnamese, a burly Hispanic who had hangover written in his bloodshot eyes, and a young black male who wore a single earring and no other bling. We were stationed around a rattling, electrically powered contraption about the size of your average Chevy Tahoe. The thing had levers, pulleys, small presses, and a long conveyer belt—lacking only a steam whistle and bell to add to the cacophony of mechanical sounds generated during the operation. The speed at which we operated was like TV's classic *I Love Lucy* scene in which Lucy and Ethel are hired to wrap chocolates coming down a conveyer belt. When the work comes at them too rapidly, creating a mess on the floor, they frantically begin stuffing chocolates in their mouths, in their hats, and down their blouses.

Our pill-packing routine went much the same way. Our hungover Hispanic coworker would feed cardboard sheets into the machine, which warped them into open-topped cartons the size of a cigar box. Soon the display cartons would come to me to fill as neatly as I could with the bottles of pills. Periodically there would be a foul-up in the operation. Cardboard would clog the machine. Bottles popped out prematurely. The conveyer belt would deliver me cartons that were upside down or misshapen, forcing me to try to fix those with one hand while grabbing bottles with the other and trying to stand them straight in the cardboard display cases.

I searched the classified ads for loftier career opportunities. The American Heart Association in Dallas wanted a public relations person with "solid writing skills." I saw me as ideal for the role. Soon I was invited in for an interview; so was another person, an attractive young woman with credentials less impressive than mine. She got the job.

Life was just one damned thing after another. I needed those damned things to turn damned better. Part-time work was no satisfactory solution, but I had no strong desire to return to the news business. What would I do if some editor took me in? Go back to writing obituaries, covering hometown beauty contests, checking the police blotter at the local jail for the latest wrecks or DWIs? Not to feign modesty, but I suspected that I was likely to be rejected as overqualified or unlikely to stick around for long, earning far less than I'd once been paid.

Any plans I might have concocted for the future suddenly were placed on hold. Brother Joe received a call from a family friend in Lubbock. Mama had suffered a spell and was taken to a hospital. Joe already was on his way from his home in Plano. I was delayed heading for Lubbock until I finished making telemarketing calls pitching purchases of burial sites for a cemetery company. It wasn't a lively sales activity, but the potential to earn a living was there. At one point sooner or later people will be involved in the business of arranging final resting places for the deceased. Death makes it a perpetual bull market.

25

Over most of a decade I had written several hundred columns that appeared in the *Lubbock Avalanche-Journal*. My mother, bless her heart, clipped every last one of them and kept them in large scrapbooks. Her practice of saving the columns from the Monday paper was something I did not know about for months. She inserted them in cellophane sleeves, which helped preserve the fragile, easily yellowed newsprint. The column-clipping routine went along with her other morning priorities: reading each obituary in the paper to be sure no familiar names escaped her notice and working the crossword puzzle in the comics pages. Both helped her mind stay sharp as well as interested in the world beyond her door. Her days of widowhood at times must have felt empty.

I would always be grateful for her saving those writings, but my first look at the scrapbooks actually made me feel a bit embarrassed. I could imagine how she would always be pulling them out to force anyone coming to the house to look at them. That I should have been self-conscious about a mother's proud display of something done by her son was odd; I myself was pleased with most of what I had written. I blew out opinions on everything from weather to world affairs. Describing a fear of the dark, roiling dust storms that often swept the plains when I was a child was written with no less intensity than thoughts about President George Herbert Walker Bush's Desert Storm war in Iraq. I wrote about high school days, times in Washington, chili cookoffs, the price of gasoline, jackrabbits on the Tech campus, the fifties country music of Lefty and Hank, and more. Mama never said anything negative about any of them. And over time those columns proved to be valuable references for me. They provided dates of key events in my life and jogged my memory about episodes I'd almost forgotten.

A worrisome message from Lubbock in late 1999 had been the wake-up call for my brother, sister, and me to seriously consider our mother's advancing age and condition. A life-threatening blood clot in her leg, which required emergency medical treatment, made us realize that at eighty years old she should no longer be living alone. By good coincidence a widowed sister-in-law was visiting with Mama at the time and called an ambulance when her leg swelled grotesquely in the night. That probably saved her life. In a way, Mama had gotten a reprieve, just as I had gotten days earlier in the Parker County courthouse. The direction of both our lives was changing.

Having no family to uproot, I was the logical choice to go live with our mother and help make easier whatever time she had left. She was frustrated at being unable to take care of herself. In February 2000 I left Fort Worth with my clothes and few apartment items and moved in with her at the home she and Coonie Horton had bought in the early sixties at 5216 14th Street in Lubbock. I took over chores she had difficulty handling. I carried out the garbage, vacuumed the carpets, operated the clothes washer and dryer, and so on. Having lived the bachelor's life for a time, I cooked well enough to prepare adequate meals for the two of us. I drove her to doctors' appointments, holding her arm as she tottered into their offices. That spared her from bringing the walker she used to steady herself while moving around the house.

It was disheartening to see the way failing vision hampered her ability to read the paper and work the daily crossword puzzle. Those were the morning routines that had helped start her day. Macular degeneration of her eyes had rendered her half-blind. I positioned the television set against the bed until the screen was only inches from her head at rest on a pillow. She would punch the numbered buttons on the remote control at random until she found the channel she wanted to watch. Her hearing was so bad that when she used the volume control she could not tell how loud the television set was on. Sometimes after having driven somewhere, I'd get out of the car in the driveway and hear the TV blaring so loudly from her bedroom you would have thought she was trying to entertain the neighborhood.

Mama soon qualified for home health care, which brought registered nurses to the house twice a week to check her condition, help her shower, change her clothes, and otherwise tend to personal things that were beyond my skills or comfort level. Their initial OASIS Baseline Assessment showed that in addition to having impaired vision and hearing, she suffered severe back pain "all the time," had "poor balance/coordination" (she'd fallen four times in two months), and was frequently constipated. OASIS, I learned, stood for Operational and Supportability Implementation System. The medical field had become so advanced and aloof from us normies that special jargon was created to identify health activities in a way we need not understand. I nevertheless understood the OASIS notation when it said that because of "memory deficit" my mother was "forgetful or gets confused about when meds were taken or what is needed." I understood that. I had seen it.

Checking records, the home health people identified thirteen different medications my mother was using, not all at once. Among them was the highly addictive painkiller Vicodin, or hydrocodone. When overused, it could have the same effect on her as hundred-proof vodka had on me. Too much rendered a person essentially drunk. She needed to be weaned off the stuff.

Such an array of health concerns might have caused another elderly person to surrender into a hopeless vegetative state. Not Mama. Her will to live had been strengthened by earlier difficulties: a childhood burn that left her with a disfiguring scar, hardships during the Great Depression years, lack of a normal education. Despite it all, she persisted in being happy, almost in a defiant kind of way.

To spare me from being housebound, we hired a part-time caregiver. Her assistance freed me to do two things that helped heal my own addled thought processes. I was able to attend AA meetings—twice daily, actually. And I enrolled in graduate school at Texas Tech, imagining that in time I might teach some wannabe journalist what I'd been taught over the course of several careers. Those activities, along with meeting responsibilities to my mother, set me on a course of maintaining seven years of continuous sobriety. That was the longest I had gone without drinking alcohol since the moment I first decided that booze made me write like Hemingway and dance like a Fred Astaire.

Returning to college gave me a new sense of vitality. Aiming for an advanced degree seemed admirable even if it was a goal with no definite

Editing *Friends of the Vietnam Center* newsletter (2003).

payoff that I could see. Perhaps I merely wanted to prove to myself, and possibly others, that the brain hadn't turned to mush despite being steeped for so long in alcohol.

Tuition costs had soared in the thirty-one years since I'd first attended Texas Technological College. On February 22, 1957, the year I graduated from Meadow High School, the campus newspaper *Toreador* reported that the Texas House in Austin had voted to double the twenty-five dollars per semester tuition to fifty dollars in the fall of 1959. That was the year I would be enrolling as a junior at Tech after finishing two years of expenses-paid schooling as a scholarship basketball player at Howard County Junior College in Big Spring. By the time I signed up for graduate school at Tech in 2000, tuition had risen to thirty-four hundred dollars a year. Unemployed while living with my mother, I took out a student loan that swelled to over ten thousand dollars by the time I received my Master of Arts degree in 2003.

As tuition had swelled, so had my girth, and students' desks seemed sized for kindergarteners. I drew a deep breath to squeeze into a seat in the School of Mass Communications. When I arrived for my first day in class, the room fell silent, some students mistaking the paunchy gray-hair entering the room to be the professor. The real prof was at least thirty years younger than my sixty-one. Some might have guessed me to be a World War II veteran in school on the GI Bill.

Tech's Vietnam Center and Archive became a focal point of my two graduate years at the university. I'd met the center's director, Dr. James R. Reckner, during my time at the *A-J*. One of my early columns described his efforts to found the center in 1989. Reckner was a military history professor and Navy veteran of the Vietnam War. He kindly brought me aboard as a student employee at the center to write and edit materials for its periodic newsletter, *Friends of the Vietnam Center*.

Having both academic and work roles at Tech strengthened a sense of optimism in me about the way life was moving. Involvement at the Vietnam Center bolstered my enthusiasm about being back in school; it turned out to be especially significant when I had to choose a subject for the thesis I was required to write under the masters degree program. Reckner had an idea. He directed me to an individual at the center who was considered the world's foremost expert on the guerrilla movement that the United States sought to defeat in the Vietnam War.

I was familiar with the name Douglas Pike. I'd heard of his studies involving the conflict in Southeast Asia. I'd seen him at one Pentagon press conference in the mid-1960s. At that time President Lyndon Johnson was escalating a war to prevent the guerrillas known as the Viet Cong from seizing control of US-backed South Vietnam. Pike was a US Foreign Service officer who spent years analyzing who and what the Viet Cong were and how they operated. His research produced an acclaimed monograph, *Viet Cong: The Organization and Techniques of the National Liberation Front of South Vietnam*.

When I met with Pike, he suggested that I write my thesis based on Viet Cong propaganda leaflets that he had collected in Vietnam. Those and other Viet Cong materials formed a major part of Tech's Vietnam Archive. Few if any scholars had delved into the collection, he said; no academic studies had been done using the propaganda items as source material.

Pike gave me a fascinating account of how he'd gotten his collection of the thousands of leaflets, cartoons, booklets, and other items out of

South Vietnam's capital of Saigon before the Communist forces took control. Congress's cutoff of military support for the war meant a retreat of US Forces from the South; in the final days there was a panic pullout of American diplomats and Vietnamese leaders who had assisted Washington in resisting a Communist takeover. With Saigon about to be overrun by North Vietnamese troops, Pike was able to arrange a hasty shipment of his treasured historical materials to the United States. The shipment took place only days before South Vietnam surrendered to North Vietnamese troops on April 30, 1975. By contrast, during the pandemonium of the American pullout, the United States was forced to abandon a more stupendous treasure: thirty tons of gold, a stash of bullion that by March 2013 would have been worth one and a half billion dollars. That was all left behind and taken over by the new Communist regime.

Following Pike's recommendation, I photocopied 114 propaganda items in the Vietnam Archive to be the focus of my research. Those I categorized according to the Vietnamese audiences at which they were aimed, identifying areas where most of the leaflets were distributed and analyzing the kinds of messages the leaflets sought to convey. The result was a thesis titled, "A Content Analysis of Viet Cong Leaflets as Propaganda, 1963–68." I was pleased with the result. The old brain still functioned fairly well, I thought. Later, I used the thesis as the basis of an article for *Vietnam* magazine, published in Leesburg, Virginia (which by coincidence was where my oldest son, Bobby, had a surveying company).

The two years of graduate studies produced another accomplishment that was no earth-shaking deal but did give me personal satisfaction. I received my one and only A-plus grade ever in college in a law of the press course taught by a retired US magistrate in Lubbock, Judge J. Q. Warnick. I was familiar with the judge's name from news involving court decisions. He knew my name from by-lines in the *Avalanche-Journal*. When grades were announced I was confident, of course, that the A-plus he gave me was based on merit and not because of my newspaper affiliation.

In 1998 the *Avalanche-Journal* had held an in-house chili cooking contest, and Judge Warnick arrived on the day of the competition to, well, *judge* the entries. I entered a pot of chili. So did *A-J* publisher

Dave Sharp and other employees of the newspaper. After my entry was declared the winner, Warnick sent a note saying—jokingly, I would like to think—that he found my chili tastier than my columns. It made me smile. At least one reader of prominence paid attention to the stuff I wrote.

Mama was pleased to see the master of arts diploma that I received in graduation ceremonies on May 17, 2003. She held the embossed cover close to her eyes to be able to read the print, just as she had to do to read obituaries in the A-J and get-well cards in the mail from friends and relatives.

I packed my black robe and cap with the tassel to take with me on a flight to Maryland to visit son Bobby and daughter-in-law Liz. Then it was on to Virginia to see Doug and his wife, Sandy. Pictures were made to record the old man's crowning achievement of 2003. Talk about looking splendid. And I wasn't feeling half-bad about myself, either.

26

We had a lively caregiver who my mother looked forward to seeing each morning. Meredith would come dancing into Mama's bedroom joking and carrying on in a merry way. "Faye, let's you and me get all dressed up tonight and go dancing, what do you think?" she would exclaim. "I need to find me some good-lookin' cowboy to do a little two-steppin'!" Mama never would have done such a thing, nor could she, at her age, but it delighted her to hear Meredith's fanciful hoopla. To hear Meredith talk, she'd enjoyed more than a few lively nights out in her time.

There was no such joviality on Monday, January 24, 2005. The date would remain firmly fixed in my mind because it was the day before my sixty-sixth birthday, and my mother's life was slipping away. For days she seemed not to recognize either me or the affable old gal who had been her good companion and attendant. Meredith felt a clamminess in Mama's feet, which she said was a bad sign. Mama's eyes were open, unblinking, staring into space as she had for hours. I sat beside the bed, clasping her hand. The fingers felt cool. "It's getting close," Meredith said. When the breathing became progressively labored, I called the hospice people who had dutifully overseen her for two years. They recommended that I advise my sister Linda in New Mexico to consider heading toward Lubbock. It was almost a five-hour drive from Ruidoso. Linda had told me she would plan to teach school as usual that Monday morning, but she had her bag packed, just in case. My telephone call caught her in the car on the way to school.

At 11:35 that morning I had my thumb pressed lightly against the vein on the underside of Mama's left wrist. Her pulse was steady but slow. I began to make notes on what was transpiring in those particular moments, but for what purpose I wasn't sure. Perhaps I thought Hospice might want a record of events. Perhaps it was a habit from years of reporting things as they occurred. Perhaps I thought that one day I'd need the information for something I might write.

At 11:41 I felt the pulse flutter. Her breathing was shallow. Her skin shone unusually pale in the bright winter sunlight through the windows. I looked up, trying to think what, if anything, should be done. Taped to the wall just over her head was a standard DNR instruction: Do Not Resuscitate. Months earlier Mama had signed the form without hesitation. Years of nursing experience had given her a keen intuition as to when certain things needed doing.

At 11:43 I felt the pulse stop. Her breathing stopped. On the side of the bed across from me Meredith slowly shook her head. I sat continuing to grasp the wrist, unable to know what I should be feeling and what I should be thinking. Suddenly Mama gasped, startling me. I felt the pulse jump once, twice, and then—. Nothing. It was finally, definitely, completely over.

Hospice of Lubbock's office was located only a block from Mama's home, in the Redbud shopping strip. Two Hospice women arrived within minutes of my call. When an ambulance came and attendants were lifting Mama's body from the bed onto a gurney, one of the Hospice women turned to me.

"I want you to leave," she said firmly.

The instruction made no sense. I was her son. I belonged there.

"I don't want you to see your mother leaving her home this way," she said.

I would be obedient only to a point. I left the bedroom but went directly to the garage and looked through the garage door window in time to see the gurney with a sheet covering the deceased, Viola Faye Horton, white female, age 84, being wheeled to the ambulance about to take her from her home for the last time.

The official certificate listed the time of my mother's death as 11:59 p.m. Whether the preciseness of the moment was based on the visual confirmation of death by the women of Hospice or based on what I reported to them after checking my notebook, I'm not sure. What I was sure about, what I would remain sure about for the rest of my life, was that my mother chose to die on January 24 and not one day later. Knowing the end was near, she made a conscious and effective decision not to die on January 25, the date of my birth. She did not want her death date to cast a shadow on my birthday observances.

People needed to be informed. I was hesitant about giving Linda and brother-in-law Mike the bad news while they were on the highway, perhaps traveling at high speed. Hospice, however, said to tell them so they could get emotionally braced for arriving at Mama's newly empty home.

It would always disturb me still that I could have felt so little emotion at that time of such great loss. I should have been overcome by grief. Instead, I had seen her body taken away beneath a sheet with as little feeling as if I were watching video of an event in someone else's life. People assured me that it was because for several months I had been preparing for that moment. Had I not been sober for six years I probably could not have possessed such stoicism. Had I been on drugs, legal or otherwise, I might have behaved in the extreme. Old Doc Seale told us at Starlite that the most grievous-acting people at funerals tended to be the mourners who were or had been on such mood helpers as Valium, Xanax or other benzos.

Both my parents were now gone, yet their spirits continued to seem quite alive in me. Their images remained vivid. Things they said would resound in my mind. It was as if they were merely gone away for a while. Long after we sold the house, some interesting happening or situation would stir a familiar urge for me to tell Mama about it, until I realized again that she was no longer there to take my call.

Several AA friends attended my mother's funeral to show support for me. Among them was a tall, attractive young brunette whom I had met only two weeks earlier at one of our AA gatherings. Dining out with a group had led to a movie date, and soon I became caught up in a relationship that would usher in a new and ultimately perplexing period of my life. Friends reminded me of the standard AA cautionary advice about not becoming emotionally attached to a member of the opposite sex in the program. One is advised to wait at least a year before entering anything resembling an intimate relationship. I wouldn't listen.

Problem number one was the fact that Kokie, as I shall call her, was half my age. Problem number two: I was ripe to act impulsively after devoting attention for so long to a dying mother. There was also another twofold problem: Kokie was incapable of being honest about almost anything, while I could not be honest with myself about why I wanted to hook up with her.

Kris Kristofferson could have been describing Kokie in one of his songs: She was a walking contradiction, partly truth and partly fiction. Actually there was hardly any truth, a considerable amount of fiction, and an abundance of outright lying in the woman's words and behavior. She told me she had just moved to Lubbock to live with her widowed mother in a new home in the fashionable new area of South Lubbock. That was only partly true. She came and went from that home according to her whims, much to the growing exasperation of her mother. She said she was an alcoholic and addict who had been in recovery for a year. That wasn't the case at all. She had attended only a few AA meetings after she and her mother settled into their upscale home. During the months I was with her, she never drank nor expressed any desire to have a drink. She was, however, a die-hard addict to drugs, and she pursued them relentlessly. Even her breasts were dishonest: siliconically enhanced.

A day came when Kokie's mother had enough of her daughter's disappearances and long absences out chasing drugs, mostly in East Lubbock. Kokie had to go, and there I was in the picture, all too willing to suggest that she move into the house that I occupied alone. It seemed a cozy arrangement for both of us, yet on an afternoon as I lay on a bed watching her hang her clothes in my closet, I had a moment of intense feeling that something about the situation was not quite right. This, I thought, might not be such a good move for me after all.

Kokie made a pretense of trying to get off drugs. She joined me in attending a few AA meetings. She was more outgoing than the usually standoffish new member and went about introducing herself. Men were impressed. Women saw phoniness. After a time with me, she enrolled in an online college program to become a medical assistant. She actually studied quite diligently, and often I sat with her at the computer doing exercises and taking tests. This went on night after night for almost six months until she obtained an eight-thousand-dollar student loan and promptly used a large chunk of it to buy a mound of crack cocaine. Her mother eventually found out that her signature had been forged in

Kokie's paperwork to obtain the loan and took action to end the education gambit. Kokie had no real desire to work at becoming a medical assistant. What she really wanted was to work her way through crack houses. She soon disappeared again to do that very thing.

AA friends nodded knowingly and smiled when I eventually admitted my foibles and opened up about my experience with Kokie. She was, I said, a sweet angel of God who happened also to be a crack cocaine addict and an accomplished streetwalker. She did what was necessary to get the drug she felt she had to have. Smoking crack cocaine eased certain inherent problems, including having an attention deficit hyperactivity disorder and being obsessive-compulsive.

I became convinced that Kokie regarded the drug as her medicine. What directly affected me most was an affliction with kleptomania that she could treat only by thievery. The stealing might be from me or from anyone else. Her mother had been forced to buy a safe to store jewelry and other valuables; otherwise, Kokie would take them and pawn them for cash to buy her medication of choice. She took items from me valuable enough to be hocked or sold to get drugs. That would happen when she failed to find all the cash she wanted in my billfold as I slept. I eventually missed a hand-held recorder I'd once used during interviews. The lawnmower went missing from the backyard. Tools vanished from the laundry room. Somehow the washer and dryer stayed put, but I came home one day to find the wide-screen TV missing from the living room.

Kokie had no car, but she had access to mine whether I gave her permission to drive it or not. Three times the car disappeared for days. The first time, I learned that police had impounded the vehicle after finding it driven by three young blacks caught shoplifting; Kokie had loaned it to them in exchange for a couple of rocks of crack cocaine. Another time I did a little detective work of my own, calling numbers Kokie had written in a notepad and tracing the car to a motel, where she was becoming fast friends with someone she'd met in the night. On the third occasion the car was abandoned with a flat tire in East Lubbock.

The question that took a long time to resolve was why I continued consorting with the woman after her repeated misdoings. A police officer younger than my youngest son tried to help me see the problem more clearly one day. We were standing on the front lawn discussing another disappearance of my car when he told me, "Mr. Horton, I believe you're a bit too old to be hanging out with a young crack addict." In other words, I was a fool. And what is that old saying? There's no fool like an old fool.

Another officer would tell me later, after the car was found yet again with Kokie still out running wild: "Sir, if you don't file charges, we're going to quit trying to track down your vehicle." I said I intended to bring charges. The police wanted a written statement from me. I said I would provide one. I delayed, but in the meantime I made efforts to keep her out of the house. She'd leave, but like a boomerang soon return. I once piled her clothes outside, intending to turn her away if she again showed her face. She came back with a plausible explanation for running off, and I relented. She'd use her feminine wiles to worm her way back in, and often that involved persuading me to smoke crack as a prelude to sex.

How ironic that I prided myself for not once drinking alcohol while Kokie was living with me, yet I repeatedly shared the crack pipe with her at the kitchen table playing cards, in the living room playing music, or in bed playing around. I never felt I was becoming addicted to crack cocaine. I was addicted to Kokie, and that addiction was a trap I could not escape without taking decisive action.

I decided to sell my mother's house—I'd bought the shares of my brother and sister—and leave Lubbock at least for a while. I bought a fifth-wheel recreational vehicle that I planned to live in when I was not towing it behind a sturdy pickup truck wherever a whim might take me. An aunt and uncle of mine spent wonderful years traveling in a trailer. A former high school classmate and his wife had sold their five-bedroom home in Lubbock and were doing the same thing. I saw taking to the highway as a good way to escape the ongoing problem I'd created for myself. Goodbye to Kokie, who was headed for jail. Hello to a better life for me.

27

I never aspired to be on radio, but a woman who stopped by my mini-newsstand in the United supermarket on Frankford Avenue told me about a certain opportunity. After hearing my brief sales pitch about subscribing to the *Lubbock Avalanche-Journal*, she asked if I'd ever done any broadcasting. No. Never considered it, as a matter of fact. She said KFYO-AM was seeking a morning news anchor. She jotted down a name and a phone number.

I pocketed her note, not really sure I would check it out. I was becoming bored selling newspaper subscriptions, even though it was a lucrative routine. Earning several hundred dollars a week part-time was fairly easy. Newspapers paid big bucks trying to sustain circulation and stop a steady bleeding of advertising revenue to television and the internet. I was doing the same subscription deals for the *A-J* as I'd just done for the *Odessa American* and before that the *Dallas Morning News*. That had kept me busy in 2007 after I junked the idea of touring America in the RV I had bought following the sale of what had been my parents' house.

I never took the fifth-wheeler on the road. I lived in it for a while at an RV park near Lubbock International Airport. But that sweet angel of God who smoked crack kept coming around looking for a place to crash and a chance to steal something. That just wouldn't do, so I sold the fifth-wheeler with the pickup to tow it and fled to Odessa in oil country south of Lubbock.

Being in Odessa was something of a homecoming. I had attended third-grade classes in elementary school there when my dad moved us to Odessa for carpenter work in the late 1940s. I was amazed at being able to locate the two-room house where we lived. The tiny place backed up to an alley where a city truck often came chugging along spraying DDT against the mosquitoes. Little brother Joe and I sometimes chased the truck, waving our arms and laughing in the chemical stuff billowing around us. The bug-killing fog didn't seem to harm us at all. Someone did speculate that perhaps it was the DDT that made me such a thick-skinned person. That hurt my feelings. I was a sensitive man.

Going to Odessa removed me from entanglement with the twisted angel in Lubbock. AA warns, however, that "geographical cures" are not long-term solutions for unresolved issues that plague us. Whatever problems people may have will follow wherever they go and unless addressed can lead them to continue drinking as a means of further escape. Consequences of past drinking episodes are forgotten. The reason, according to the Big Book, is that alcoholics "are unable, at certain times, to bring into our consciousness with sufficient force the memory of the suffering and humiliation of even a week or a month ago. We are without defense against the first drink."

On a bright, sunny day in Odessa, facing no big crisis in life, I couldn't resist a sudden urge to return to my apartment, kick back in the recliner, listen to a little music, read the paper, and relax with a crisp Beefeater martini on the rocks. It seemed such a harmless thing, but did I consider that I would be ending seven years of good sobriety? I did not, and soon I found myself buying the necessary gin and vermouth in a liquor store near the H-E-B supermarket where I'd been selling subscriptions for the *Odessa American*. I didn't mean to get terribly drunk; it wasn't the worst drinking I ever did. But one Beefeater led to another, and then more, setting me up for a series of boozy days and weeks to come.

You can hear it said in the halls, church basements, clubs, and other places where meetings of Alcoholics Anonymous are held: Exposure to AA can really mess up your enjoyment of drinking. I tired of the daily habit of getting liquored up, driving at risk of being arrested, feeling increasingly depressed, and realizing whenever I managed to be truthful with myself that it led to no good end. I did not want to lose hope that life still held good things for me. I knew I had to stop what I was doing, and stop it soon. A six-month lease ended in June, less than two months away. I would drink the time away, point my little Buick Skylark toward Lubbock, and get back into an AA routine.

No one scoffed at me that Monday morning when I walked into the Hub of the Plains AA club at 34th Street and Memphis Avenue in Lubbock. AA people welcome back the relapser. Knowing I had once been a dutiful member, they were a bit surprised, but they had witnessed many times the cunning, baffling, powerful appeal of alcohol over people. Even old-timers with fifteen, twenty, or more years of sobriety inexplicably choose to "go back out" for new attempts at controlled drinking. True alcoholics are incapable of controlling their drinking. They wind up coming back to AA, beaten down, tail between their legs. They come back, that is, if they've managed to survive the continuing binges.

Time between careers might be like the holding pattern of some airliner awaiting clearance to land. What seems a destination may be only a refueling stop on the way to somewhere else. In my case, newspaper subscription sales turned out to be the holding pattern that preceded a venture into radio news broadcasting.

At first it was daunting.

"Good morning, at six-oh-three, I'm Bob Horton" was the easiest part of the newscast that began the day on 790 KFYO-AM in Lubbock. The rougher part was the writing and recording of the two- to three-minute newscasts that were to run every half-hour. Assembling those brief segments sounded simple enough, but the clock worked against the ability to freshen each newscast by introducing new items or updating others.

Once written and recorded, a newscast was electronically transferred at a certain time to a computer, which directed its broadcast into a designated time slot. If the news anchor missed the transfer deadline, the computer automatically rebroadcast the news of a previous day. Listeners would be left shaking their heads in confusion upon hearing what was easily recognized as old news. I suspect that I set heads to spinning a number of times in my first weeks at the microphone. Any blunder I made could be heard by more than just people around Lubbock. KFYO reached listeners in Amarillo, Abilene, Midland, Odessa, as south as far as Ozona, and the eastern New Mexico cities of Hobbs and Clovis. Some forty-five thousand would hear the station through online streaming. The temptation is to think that most people failed to catch less blatant errors, such as incorrect verb tenses. But hear they did—they'd call in saying so—when something grievously wrong came out of my mouth such as, "First responders today rescued a driver from the wreckage of his car using the Jaws of Death." Yes, yes, I know: Jaws of *Life!*

News operations manager Rob Snyder patiently trained me to take over as morning news anchor. I sat beside him for a month observing how he updated scripts from previous days and what was done in the recording and editing of audio. In the broadcast studio was a bank of machines that had dials with wiggly hands showing the varying volume of the sounds and screens with glowing numbers and lined charts. The combination of it had the place looking like the cockpit of a big airliner. Had it been an airliner, I would have crashed it from making so many mistakes during my early days of running the show. At times I was so challenged that I felt I should quit. Better to quit than be fired, I figured. Snyder probably didn't want that. He'd only find himself spending another month babysitting some other trainee.

My first Lubbock newscast went out at 6:03 a.m. on KFYO, but I rolled out of bed at 2:30 a.m. to be in the studio by 3:30 to prepare four newscasts for the company's sister stations, KLUB-FM and KIXS-FM in Victoria near the Gulf of Mexico. Having once been accustomed to awakening to a rooster's crow on farms in West Texas, I had no difficulty arising at such an early hour. The Victoria newscasts ran at six, seven, eight, and nine o'clock. I also delivered Lubbock's KOOL98-FM newscast.

Six months elapsed before I began to feel confident in the radio routine. Despite the tight deadlines, I found myself able to step outside occasionally during my six-hour shift to smoke a cigarette. I needed those respites from the pressure. Even so, I had to remain mindful of the clock and constantly think of fresh items to weave into upcoming newscasts.

I never really had a strong interest in being in radio work. Print journalism was the direction I was pointed as early as my high school days. Seeing a talent for writing, my mother planted the idea that I should be a newspaper reporter. When I was a senior, she and an English teacher took me to a journalism seminar at Texas Tech, where one of the speakers was Jay Harris, the A-J's night managing editor. Harris would later become my boss when I worked at the paper while attending Tech. I would often hear newspaper people dismiss radio guys as "rip and read" artists who didn't gather the news but merely stripped stories off the Associated Press wire and shouted them on the air. I learned there was more to radio than that.

Radio had my attention well before newspapers and long before the advent of television. I remember Grandad Horton playing the radio in the kitchen so he could hear the weather forecast and livestock reports on the price of cotton, pork belly futures, and such as coffee was brewing. I recall sitting with my father listening to a boxing match in 1947 between heavyweight champion Joe Louis and a light heavyweight challenger named Billy Conn. Daddy sat hunched on the edge of a cane-bottomed chair cheering for Conn, but "the Pittsburgh Kid" lost by a knockout. I think Daddy had a bet on Conn to beat the "Brown Bomber."

When I was about nine years old and we were living in Odessa, I appeared on an afternoon program for children. Odessa's radio station KOSA had a contest for youngsters to name the program they listened to most. I regularly listened to *Terry and the Pirates* and a show featuring cowboy movie star Tom Mix. But the postcard I sent in said that what I enjoyed most was a certain scary program that made my hair "stand on end." Mine was the winning entry, and I was invited on the show to receive an album of 78 rpm records by cowboy actor and singer Tex Ritter, along with a year's subscription for a comic book featuring two new heroes, Batman and Robin. *Holy moly!* If I'd saved those early issues they would have become worth a small fortune.

Such memories made me have some early affinity for radio. Being a news anchor afforded an opportunity in later years to dust off and reuse writing skills I'd developed in other media roles.

I continued assembling and announcing the news on KFYO for almost six years until a personal writing project that I had been pursuing after hours began to take on greater meaning. It started when my younger son, Doug, saw a job résumé I had prepared as I looked ahead to my seventies. I could see that I needed a job to have a paycheck supplementing a modest Social Security draw. Doug, glancing over the places I had worked, said, "Daddy I didn't know you did all that. You should write it and tell us about it."

Only then did I think seriously of producing something of a memoir. I saw that as likely to be of far more value to Doug and his brother Bob-

Flying from Virginia to Lubbock, *right to left*, youngest son Doug Horton, his son Carter, and Bobby Don Horton (1996).

Oldest son Bobby Don with his mother, Sherry Horton, visiting Maryland.

by than the meager inheritance they could expect once I left the scene. I realized, too, that my sons would gain little from a mere recitation of places I had lived and positions I had held. They might benefit considerably, though, if I also described things I had experienced, explaining as best I could what I had learned from those experiences. In order to devote full attention to the writing I told KFYO operations manager Snyder that I was resigning, and why, and walked away from radio in February 2013.

Epilogue

I left the *Lubbock Avalanche-Journal* in 1961 as a lightly experienced twenty-two-year-old reporter who had been offered a better news job, practically out of the blue, with the Associated Press. I was assigned to AP bureaus first in Tennessee and later in Washington, DC. The moves were more than advances in a profession that I had begun thinking of pursuing as early as my teenage years. They represented unconscious adherence to a mother's frequent admonition to get an education, leave the farm, and "make something of yourself."

There was a slight problem for me in trying to do what Mama often suggested. I did not know who or what "something" was supposed to mean. The idea nevertheless seemed important, so off I meandered along roads that for years kept me far beyond the dusty plains of West Texas. I became something I aspired to be: a correspondent in Washington covering major news events emanating from the Pentagon, Congress, the State Department, the White House, and all those important places in the nation's capital. I also became something my mother never had in mind for me. I became an alcoholic.

There came a time when, after years of pushing, I no longer felt a need to demonstrate what I could accomplish in the world beyond West Texas. I had proven all I needed to prove, with one exception: a willingness and an ability to stop drinking. The new challenge before me was learning how to live a life of some value to family, friends and society at large.

Finally I found that I was making progress. As of 2016 I was still attending meetings of Alcoholics Anonymous, still truthfully claiming a sobriety date stretching back for nine years. I felt more at ease with myself. I had a sense of hope about the future.

When I spoke in meetings with other AA members, I introduced myself

Cheering Texas Tech's Red Raiders (2013).

this way: "I'm Bob Horton and I am an alcoholic. My dry date is September twenty-fourth, two thousand seven. That's not my first dry date, but I'm okay with that today. I had to learn what I needed to learn when I needed to learn it. I'm glad to be here alive, sober, and fairly sober-minded. I owe that to this program, you people, and the help of a Higher Power."

Alcoholics develop their own personal styles of introductions when sharing their stories in open discussions at AA meetings. One might say simply, "I'm Hawkeye, dry twenty-six years. Glad to be here." Another: "I'm Janie. I'm an alcoholic. I'm only here to listen." A more imaginative way is sometimes heard, such as: "I'm an alcoholic, my *problem* is Howard. I haven't found it necessary to drink alcohol or light a joint since November tenth nineteen-sixty-six."

AA members in other states do not give a "dry date" preceding their remarks. I've wondered whether the Texas habit of announcing the day the drinking stopped comes off as a bit of braggadocio. Perhaps it should not. Announcing a dry date informs newcomers which members have been in recovery longest and who therefore might be among the wiser heads in discussions about recovery.

I began attending AA meetings in Washington, DC, in the 1980s. Eventually I was giving what I thought was a valid explanation about how I became seriously dependent on alcohol for changing the way I felt. When I first arrived in the nation's capital, I said, I drank to ease an insecurity about my performance as a young reporter. The drinking became something of a celebratory routine as I grew more confident about competing head to head with media veterans. In time, a prideful arrogance about the success I saw myself achieving led me to drink even more heartily. In my mind I became quite an important man.

I understand now that I triggered an alcoholic tendency before ever arriving in Washington. It happened when I took that first drink as a teenager and instantly felt on equal terms with older classmates and teammates. Drinking helped me to fit in. Later, the striving to be on a level with others became a futile effort to be smarter than, faster than, better than anyone else. That, I had to learn through experience, is not possible. Somewhere someone else will always be smarter, faster, and better than Bob. AA eventually taught me that I needed to be at ease with who I am, where I am. Just being Bob, with whatever talents and flaws God endowed me, could be good as gold. *Fine as wine*.

Learning what is required to correct a misguided way of life has not been a simple process for me, and the learning does continue. Over the years I've attended hundreds of AA meetings with thousands of other people struggling with the same kinds of addiction problems that plagued me. Almost every friend I have is to be found in AA meetings. I owe a debt of gratitude to them and to the AA program for showing me how to stay sober and be able to enjoy the serenity that comes with sobriety. I can repay that debt only by staying active in AA and thus in a position to share with another suffering individual what has been freely shared with me.

The final step of AA's twelve-step program tells members this: "Having had a spiritual awakening as the result of these steps, we tried to carry this message to other alcoholics and to practice these principles in all our affairs." What are those principles, a newcomer will ask? They include honesty about one's powerlessness over alcohol, courage for making a searching and fearless moral inventory of oneself, and spirituality, seeking through prayer and meditation to improve a conscious contact with God as one understands Him, "praying only for knowledge of His will for us and the power to carry it out."

In May 2013 a person in the twelve-step program—call her Misty—

Bobby Horton with Disney animated character Elsa (2016).

learned that I was putting the story of my life and times on paper. She asked me how the writing was going. She and her husband had years of sobriety and were prospering after overcoming addictions they'd had before getting married. I told her I was approaching the final chapter.

"What is your conclusion going to be?" she asked.

I laughed. I didn't know that my story would have any major "conclusion" or soul-stirring moral at the end. I did have in mind a vague idea about what I thought I might put down as the final lines. They were to go something like this: "And so life went on. We did not live happily ever after but we lived. Even though we all would soon be forgotten, even though everything we said or did or thought we knew eventually would be swept away, we could take comfort in the fact that we had endured. We survived. We did live."

Misty did not think much of such an ending. "We're sober, you know!" she exclaimed. "We're living happily ever after *right now*!"

Her reaction left me perplexed. I needed to rethink what I had in mind.

That night I went to bed trying to decide what would be the best conclusion for the story. When I awoke I still didn't have it, but I was still alive, still above ground, still having the opportunity to seek a solution. Bright slits in window blinds made me aware that the sun had risen again as it always had. A new day dawned and once more I could be grateful for not feeling that obsession for pouring alcohol into my body to banish a fear or some other unknown demon.

A thought occurred to me then that seemed to make sense. Feeling assured that the wicked obsession about drinking had truly been banished might indeed be enough to keep a man living happily ever after. Mama Faye Horton could probably agree with that.

Bob Horton in 2016

Index

Page numbers in *italic* indicate images.

About the Author

Bob Horton has been in the news business for more than fifty years. In 1966 he received the Top Reporting Performance Award from the Associated Press Managing Editors organization, and in 1968 he and an AP cohort were nominated for a Pulitzer Prize for general coverage of the Pentagon during the Vietnam War. Today he is a radio news anchor with shows in Lubbock and Victoria, Texas. He lives in Lubbock.